CHRONICLES OF THE ROMAN WORLD

ANCIENT ROME

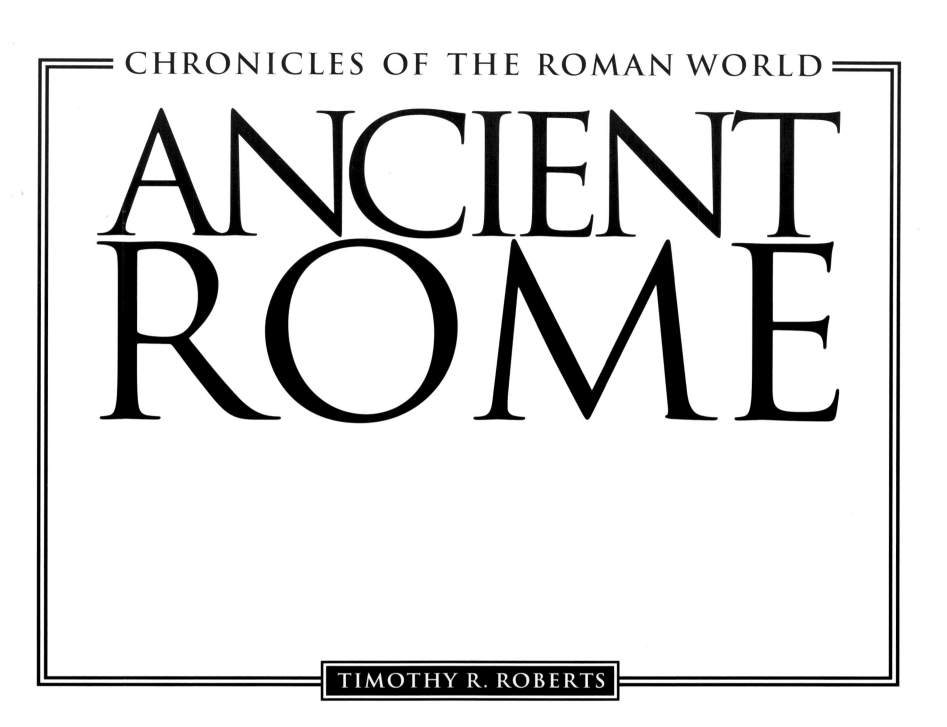

CHRONICLES OF THE ROMAN WORLD

ANCIENT ROME

TIMOTHY R. ROBERTS

MetroBooks

MetroBooks

An Imprint of Friedman/Fairfax Publishers

Library of Congress Cataloging-in-Publication Data

Roberts, Timothy Roland, 1942-
    Ancient Rome / Timothy R. Roberts.
        p. cm. — (Chronicles of the Roman world)
    Includes bibliographical references and index.
    ISBN 1-56799-724-4 (alk. paper)
    1. Rome—History. 2. Rome—Pictorial works. I. Title. II. Series.

    DG209 .R54 2000
    937—dc21
        99-462290

Editors: Alexandra Bonfante-Warren, Celeste Sollod, and Susan Lauzau
Art Director: Jeff Batzli
Designers: Christina Grupico and Jennifer O'Connor
Photography Editors: Jennifer L. Bove and Erin Feller
Production Manager: Camille Lee

Color separations by Fine Arts Repro House Co., Ltd.
Printed in Hong Kong by Sing Cheong Printing Company Ltd.

10 9 8 7 6 5 4 3 2 1

For bulk purchases and special sales, please contact:
Friedman/Fairfax Publishers
Attention: Sales Department
15 West 26th Street
New York, NY 10010
212/685-6610 FAX 212/685-1307

Visit our website:
www.metrobooks.com

DEDICATION

For the indefatigable supporter of our family,

my mother, Garnavieve Irene Beeson Roberts

CONTENTS

A Timeline of Ancient Rome

THE MONARCHY 753 B.C.–509 B.C.

April 21, 753 The legendary founding of the city of Rome

753–715 Legendary dates of the reign of King Romulus

715–673 Legendary dates of the reign of King Numa Pompilius

673–641 Legendary dates of the reign of King Tullus Hostilius

641–617 Legendary dates of the reign of King Ancus Marcius

617–579 Legendary dates of the reign of Lucius Tarquinius Priscus

579–534 Legendary dates of the reign of Servius Tullius

534–509 Legendary dates of the reign of Superbus Tarquinius Priscus

509 Founding of the Roman Republic

THE REPUBLIC 509 B.C.–27 B.C.

499 Romans defeat the Latin League at Battle of Lake Regillus

491 Roman renegade Gnaeus Marcius Coriolanus nearly conquers Rome

482 Aequi and Veientes invade Roman Republic

477 Romans lose Battle of Cremera River

455 Plebeians allowed consular powers

451 The Twelve Tablets written

c. 450 Gaulish Celts invade Italy

443 Censors first elected

405–396 Roman siege of the Etruscan city of Veii

387 Gauls subjugate Etruria and lay siege to their city of Clusium

386 Gauls force Romans to pay ransom for their city

367 Praetors appointed

366 Creation of the Comitia Tributa

343–337 First Samnite War

338 Gaius Maenius defeats Volsci

328–321 Second Samnite War. Five-year truce begins after Roman defeat at the Battle of the Caudine Forks

316–311 Second Samnite War resumes

298–290 Third Samnite War

287 The Lex Hortensia passed; plebian assemblies allowed to pass laws without Senatorial approval

283 Gauls defeated at Battle of Lake Vadimon

272 Rome signs a treaty of friendship with Ptolemy II

264–241 First Punic War

229–146 Conquest of Greece

218–202 Second Punic War

146–143 Third Punic War

133–121 Reforms of the Gracchi Brothers

114–113 Roman armies beaten by Celts

107 Gaius Marius chosen consul; defeats Jugurtha in north Africa.

104–101 Marius campaigns against the Celts

90–88 War against the Italian allies

87 Lucius Cornelius Sulla campaigns against Mithridates VI in Asia

80 Sulla elected consul

73–71 Spartacus leads revolt of Italian slaves

70 Gnaeus Pompeius Magnus (Pompey the Great) and Marcus Lucinius Crassus elected co-consuls

67 Pompey campaigns in western Asia

60 Formation of the First Triumvirate: Gaius Julius Caesar, Pompey, and Crassus

58–51 Julius Caesar campaigns in Gaul

52 Caesar besieges Alesia in Gaul

49 Caesar returns to Rome, crosses the Rubicon, and begins a civil war with Pompey

48 Battle of Pharsalus; Pompey flees to Egypt and is murdered

47–44 Caesar supreme in Rome; murdered on March 15, 44

43–37 Second Triumvirate formed: Marcus Aemilius Lepidus, Gaius Octavius Thurins (Octavius), and Marcus Antonius (Antony)

42 Marcus Antonius and Octavius defeat Caesar's assassins at Philippi in Greece

38 Virgil publishes his *Bucolica* and begins his literary career

36 Antony marries Cleopatra VII

31 Battle of Actium; Antony defeated

30 Antony and Cleopatra commit suicide after Octavius' victory. Horace publishes his *Satires*, which launches his career

29 Octavius returns to Rome

27 On January 16 the Senate votes to give Octavius the title *Augustus*, or "consecrated one." His elevation as the first Roman emperor signals the end of the Roman Republic. Livy begins *De urbe condita*

THE EMPIRE: 27 B.C. TO 476 A.D.

22 The Roman army defeats the Ethiopian army of Queen Candace

14 Ovidius publishes *Amores*

9 The Roman Senate votes the Altar of Peace (*Ara pacis*) to Augustus

4 B.C. Jesus born

9 The Germans annihilate a Roman army under Publius Quinctilius Varus

14 Augustus dies

14–37 Reign of Tiberius Claudius Nero (Tiberius)

31 Attempted coup against Tiberius by Lucius Aelius Sejanus

30 Pontius Pilate, procurator of Judea, orders the execution of Jesus

37–41 Reign of Gaius Caesar Augustus Germanicus (Caligula)

41–54 Reign of Tiberius Claudius Drusus Nero Germanicus (Claudius)

43 Roman legions invade Britain

54–68 Reign of Nero Claudius Drusus Germanicus Caesar (Nero)

56 Tribunes forbidden by law to counter the actions of the consuls or the Senate

64 The Great Fire of Rome

66 Revolt begins in Judea against Roman Rule

68 Nero commits suicide; three men use military force to try for the throne, Servius Sulpicius Galba, Gaius Julius Vindex, and Titus Flavius Sabinus Vespasianus; Vespasianus wins and becomes emperor

69–79 Reign of Vespasianus

73–74 Roman armies invade northern Germany

79 Mt. Vesuvius erupts and buries Pompeii

77–84 Romans conquer most of Britain

79–81 Reign of Titus Flavius Vespasianus (Titus)

81–96 Reign of Titus Flavius Domitianus (Domitian)

85–89 Dacians invade Roman Empire

96–98 Reign of Marcus Cocceius Nerva (Nerva) begins the Era of the Five Good Emperors, which lasts 84 years until the death of Marcus Aurelius Antoninus

98–117 Reign of Marcus Ulpius Trajanus (Trajan)

101–107 The Dacian Wars add another province to the Empire

113–117 The Parthian Wars

117–138 Reign of Publius Aelius Hadrianus (Hadrian)

131 The Praetor's Edict allows the emperor to rule by imperial decree

132–135 Revolt of the Jews under Bar Kokhba

138–161 Reign of Titus Aurelius Antoninus (Antoninus Pius)

161–180 Reign of Marcus Annius Verus (Marcus Aurelius)

166–175 Barbarians invaders sweep across the northern Roman frontier, and Marcus Aurelius spends the rest of his reign fighting them

167 Roman troops returning from campaigns against the Parthians bring plague to Italy

180–192 The reign of Lucius Aelius Aurelius Commodus (Commodus)

193–211 Reign of Septimius Severus

197–198 Romans campaign in Parthia

211–284 Of the twenty–seven emperors who reigned during this period, seventeen are murdered, two commit suicide, three die in battle, one is captured by the enemy, and only four die in bed

284–305 Reign of Gaius Aurelius Valerius Diocletianus; Diocletian reorganizes the army, civil service, taxation, and economy of the Empire; for administrative purposes, divides the Empire into two parts, each ruled by an emperor assisted by a junior Caesar

305–306 Reign of Aurelius Valerius Constantius I

306–337 Reign of Flavius Valerius Aurelius Constantinus (Constantine I)

313 Constantine issues the Edict of Milan, which extends recognition to the Christians

330 Constantine's new capital on the shores of the Bosphorus becomes known as Constantinople

337–361 Empire ruled in succession by the sons of Constantine, Constantine II, Constantius, and Constans

361–363 Reign of the emperor Flavius Claudius Julianus (Julian) who temporarily restores paganism as the dominant religion of the Empire

363–379 The Empire ruled by a succession of weak emperors

378 The Visigoths defeat a Roman Army at Adrianople, kill the emperor, Valens, and pillage the Balkans; the rest of the Empire falls into chaos

379–395 Reign of Theodosius I, called the Great; he restores order, but on his death formally divides the Empire between his two sons Arcadius and Honorius. The division weakens the Empire

395–476 A succession of weak emperors rules over a disintegrating Empire

406 Romans evacuate Britain

408 The Visigoth king Alaric invades Italy

410 Alaric sacks Rome

429 Vandals seize Roman province of Africa and set up an independent Empire

451 Attila, king of the Huns, invades Gaul

451 The Roman general Aëtius defeats Attila at the Battle of Chalons in Gaul

453 Attila tries to sack Rome but fails; Pope Leo I leads the defense of the city

455 Rome sacked by the German Gaiseric and his Vandals

455–476 The Roman Emperors become puppets of German barbarians

476 Romulus Augustulus, the last Roman emperor, deposed; he sends the imperial paraphernalia to the Roman emperor in the East, at Constantinople

A Timeline of Ancient Rome

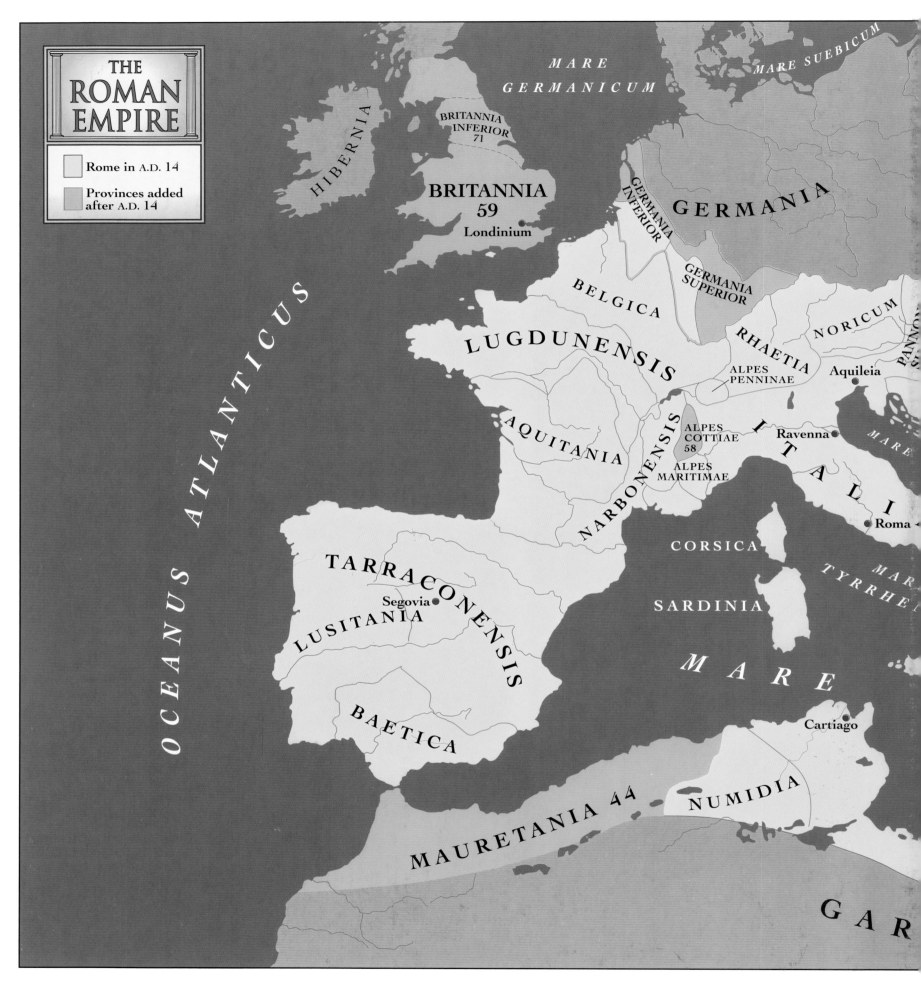

THE
ROMAN
EMPIRE

Rome in A.D. 14

Provinces added
after A.D. 14

MARE
GERMANICUM

MARE SUEBICUM

HIBERNIA

BRITANNIA
INFERIOR
71

BRITANNIA
59
Londinium

GERMANIA
INFERIOR

GERMANIA
SUPERIOR

GERMANIA

BELGICA

NORICUM

O C E A N U S   A T L A N T I C U S

LUGDUNENSIS

RHAETIA

ALPES
PENNINAE

PANNO

Aquileia

AQUITANIA

ALPES
COTTIAE
58

ALPES
MARITIMAE

NARBONENSIS

I T A L I

Ravenna

MARE

Roma

TARRACONENSIS

Segovia

CORSICA

SARDINIA

TYRRHE

MARE

LUSITANIA

BAETICA

M A R E

Cartiago

MAURETANIA 44

NUMIDIA

G A R

MARE CASPIUM

SARMATAE

BOSPORAN KINGDOM

COLCHIS

ALBANIA

MATAE

PONTUS EUXINUS

ARMENIA 114-117

PARTHIANS

DACIA 106

BITHNIA AND PONTUS 107

ASSYRIA 116-117

MOESIA

CAPPADOCIA 17

COMMAGENE

MESOPOTAMIA 115-117

Byzantium

THRACIA 46

ASIA

GALATIA

CILICIA

SYRIA

CUM

MACEDONIA

PAMPHYLIA

COELE 200

ICUM

Ephesus

LYCIA 43

CYPRUS

PHOENICIA 200

EPIRUS 140

Athenae

RHODUS

JUDEA 44

Sparta

CRETA

ARABIA 106

INTERNUM

Alexandria

SINUS ARABICUS

RICA

CYRENAICA

AEGYPTUS

ANTES

The Roman Empire

INTRODUCTION

*Nescire autem quid ante-
quam natus sis acciderit,
id est semper esse puerum*
(NOT TO KNOW WHAT HAPPENED BEFORE YOU WERE BORN
IS TO BE FOREVER A CHILD.)
—MARCUS TULLIUS CICERO (106–43 B.C.)

Rome in the Ancient World

THE ROMAN EMPIRE HAS been in the past now for at least fifteen hundred years, and yet it remains the best known and most easily recognized of all the civilizations of the ancient world. Even though many people may not be able to differentiate among the Monarchy, the Republic, or the Empire periods of Roman history, most educated laymen know a few rudimentary facts about Caesar, the Tiber, legions, Cleopatra, or Nero. They may even know that aspects of our legal tradition come from ancient Rome, as do basic principles that pertain to engineering and architecture. Many may even feel comfortable enough to venture an opinion as to why the Roman Empire fell—because of corruption, too much government, homosexuals, sin, or lead poisoning, all of which have enjoyed popularity as possible causes at one time or another.

The fact that many people know something about Rome is not surprising, because in addition to the contributions that ancient Rome passed on to the modern world, many people have a vague realization of the hugeness of the Roman world and the diversity of its subjects. The Roman world stretched, at its fullest extent, for thirty-four hundred miles (5,470km) from the Atlantic Ocean to the head of the Persian Gulf and for fourteen hundred miles (2,252km) from the coastal plains of North Africa to the border of Scotland. This tremendous size makes Rome as awe-inspiring to the people of our era as it was to the people of the ancient world that Rome dominated.

The Roman Empire contained a bewildering number of different cultures and groups, people who were governed effectively by Rome's single government. Somehow, the Empire was able to harmonize into an effective political union that included not only rude, woad- (a blue clay that they smeared on themselves) covered savages from what is today Great Britain but also sophisticated Greeks, Babylonians, and Egyptians, along with all the other people in between. Rome did not just collect these people into one Empire, but truly enhanced their lives and gave them better opportunities than they had ever had at any other time in the ancient world. For ancient Rome placed few impediments in the way of people who were not native-born Italian Romans. A Spaniard, an Arab, a Gaul, or an Illyrian had just as much chance of rising to fame, fortune, and prominence in the Roman Empire as a native Roman from the imperial city itself. Even the office of emperor was open to any citizen of the Empire who had enough luck, talent, and courage to seize the office.

Even with that most perverse of human institutions—slavery—the Romans did not discriminate. Throughout the Empire, slavery was never fastened on one specific group or race of people. Anyone unlucky enough to be captured in war or born to slave parents was a slave. Even then, slavery was not necessarily a permanent condition; many slaves earned their freedom or were granted their freedom and could then rise to positions of importance within Roman society.

Perhaps the most impressive aspect of the ancient Roman Empire was that the government preserved the general well-being of such a great number of cultures and people over such a large area. The magnificent Roman army not only maintained order within the Empire; it guarded a frontier that stretched east

Rome in the Ancient World

through Europe to the Persian Gulf and west across North Africa to the Atlantic. The Roman army effectively policed the interior of the Empire and ensured that food and the necessities of life flowed freely and abundantly from one end to the other. Amazingly, the army controlled this vast area of more than 1,700,000 square miles (4,403,000 sq km) with only 450,000 troops—a startling feat when one considers that the United States was unable to win a war in South Vietnam, a country of barely sixty-seven thousand square miles (173,530 sq km), with an army of 500,000 soldiers. Even more amazing is the fact that the same Roman army, always outnumbered, faced repeated attacks by a variety of invaders along the whole line of the frontier for the last three hundred years of the Empire's existence.

There is, finally, another surprisingly admirable aspect of Rome's great power, for this huge state, built and guarded by its professional army, did not develop out of a selfish desire for conquest or wealth. Rome's expansion from a tiny sixth-century B.C. enclave on the banks of the Tiber to a world empire in the first century A.D. resulted largely from a never-ending attempt to ensure its own security against neighbors bent on its destruction. One might almost say that Rome conquered the Mediterranean Basin in self-defense. From Rome's earliest wars against the Etruscans through the repeated wars with Carthage, Macedonia, Syria, and Persia, the primary goal of the Roman state was to ensure a safe and stable environment for Rome. For instance, between 217 and 146 B.C., in a series of wars against the Macedonian kingdom of Philip V and his son Perseus, the Romans sought to protect Roman mercantile interests in the Adriatic Sea while at the same time preserving the balance of power in Greece among the small city-

states; this was necessary because any one of them could have threatened Rome's power along the Adriatic coast. After each successful war, however, the Romans withdrew from Greece, only to be forced to return when, once more, the Macedonians seemed to suggest a threat to Roman interests. Only at the end of a fourth war did the Romans decide to permanently annex a portion of Greece.

Certainly during the long periods of the Roman Republic (509–27 B.C.) and the Roman Empire (27 B.C.–A.D. 476) one could find some instances of greedy selfishness. Yet in the main, Rome's primary motive in war appeared to be self-protection rather than naked imperialism. Here, again, Rome's experience is different from that of other ancient Mediterranean empires in Egypt and Greece. In this regard as well as in others, Rome's uniqueness is surely the reason that for so many years since its fall, people have been drawn to study both its mistakes and its triumphs.

Below: In the nineteenth century, when Alexandre Cabanel painted this portrait of Cleopatra VII (69–30 B.C.), people viewed her as a seductive temptress who addled the wits of Mark Antony and Julius Caesar. Such a view obscures the fact that both men saw Egypt as an important source of wealth to fund their political ambitions, and Cleopatra as an able ally.

Rome in the Ancient World

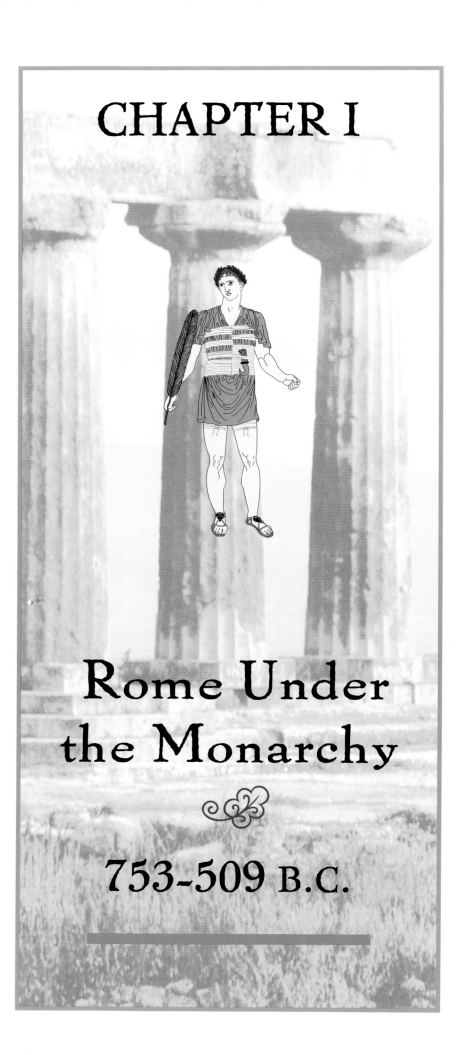

CHAPTER I

Rome Under the Monarchy

753-509 B.C.

ROMULUS AND REMUS

The history of Rome begins with a legend: Romulus and Remus, the twin sons of the god Mars, left Alba Longa, the city of their birth, and traveled ten miles (16km) north to build their own city, which eventually became Rome. Earlier, in Alba Longa, they had restored their uncle Numitor to the throne that had been illegally taken from him. After such a noble act, the two brothers could have lived their lives in ease in Alba Longa, but a spirit of adventure and a desire to mold their own destinies drove them to leave that city with a young and adventurous segment of the population and move to a site with seven hills on the east bank of the Tiber River.

At this point along the river, an island diverted the current, creating a natural crossing point. The east bank of this ford was dominated by seven hills. Four of them, the Quirinal, Viminal, Esquiline, and Caelian, were spurs of an ancient volcanic ridge that lay to the east. The other three hills, the Palatine, Aventine, and Capitoline, stand separately from these spurs. In the eighth century B.C., when Romulus and Remus arrived, all seven of the hills were prominent and easily distinguishable from one another. Over the centuries since the city was founded, however, the ravines that separated these hills have disappeared because of the accumulation of rubble, trash, and ruins. Today it is impossible to distinguish where one hill begins and another ends, except for the Capitoline, which is still evident. From earliest times, this steep hill formed a natural defense point. When

the first settlers arrived in the area, the bottoms of the ravines as well as the area between the hills and the river were marshes that were natural breeding grounds for malaria. When Romulus and Remus first arrived at the site, it was uninhabited except for a village of Sabines on the Quirinal, the most northern of the seven hills.

When the two brothers arrived, they immediately set to work building separate fortified villages. Remus built on the Aventine and Romulus on the Palatine, but while this construction was going on, the two brothers fell into a dispute over which of them should be king. When the dispute became violent, Romulus fatally struck Remus. Romulus became king, and the emerging city was named Rome in his honor. Ancient historians assigned Romulus' ascendancy and the founding of the city to a date that corresponds to our April 21, 753 B.C., although there is absolutely no way to confirm the accuracy of this. (In the Roman calendar, this date was considered 1 A.U.C., as they counted their years *ab urbe condita*, which means from the founding of the city.) Archaeological excavations indicate that the site of Rome was inhabited long before—at least as far back as 1000 B.C.

Little evidence supports the legend of Romulus and Remus. A more tenable truth is perhaps that the people of Alba Longa and those of the later city of Rome were at one time the same people; we can also assume with some certainty that when these Latin people arrived at the site of Rome, there was already a Sabine settlement on the Quirinal. Archaeology also supports the legend that one of the first settlements in the area, after that on the Quirinal, was on the Palatine, and that there was a fortress on the Capitoline in the city's earliest times. As for Romulus, he was probably created by Roman historians of the fourth century B.C. to explain their origins; likewise, Remus was probably also a fictional character whom the plebeians, or lower class in Rome, created as a counterpart to Romulus.

THE SABINE WOMEN

The legends that have arisen about the time period of Romulus' reign, which supposedly lasted from 753 to 715 B.C., perhaps contain some historic material. Archaeology confirms, for instance, that at an early date the Romans living on the Palatine joined with the Sabines who lived on the Quirinal. This historical event may be reflected in the famous tale of the capture of the Sabine women, related by the Roman historian Livy (59 B.C.–A.D. 17). According to the story, once settled in his new city on the Palatine,

Romulus became concerned that his followers had not brought enough women with them from Alba Longa. He therefore proposed an alliance with the Sabines, hoping they would allow the Romans to intermarry with Sabine women. The Sabines, however, contemptuously declined any association with these newcomers. Romulus appeared to accept this rejection, but later he persuaded the Sabines to attend a feast on the Palatine to celebrate the *Consualia*, a festival in honor of the god Neptune. During the feast, the Romans drank only wine that had been cut with water, but they gave their guests, the Sabines, undiluted wine. The Romans feigned drunkenness to encourage the Sabines to drink more, and when the Sabines were thoroughly besotted, the Romans seized the unmarried Sabine women and threw their drunken menfolk outside the city gates.

Above: Scenes from Rome's mythological past were popular subjects in the sixteenth and seventeenth centuries, as seen in Peter Paul Reubens' (1577–1640) *The Rape of the Sabine Women*. In this case the term *rape* refers not to a sexual act but to the forcible kidnapping of the women.

The Romans had every honorable intention toward the captured Sabine women, begged their forgiveness for kidnapping them, and lost no time marrying them. The Sabine men were understandably distressed and, when they sobered up, launched an attack on the Romans, who had in the meantime fortified themselves on the Capitoline. During the siege, however, the Sabine women, assured of the honorable intentions of the Romans, fell in love with their new husbands and appealed to their Sabine fathers and brothers to forgive the abduction. The women pointed out that they stood to lose no matter which side won: "If you fight and kill our new husbands, we are the losers, and if the Romans fight and kill you, we are also the victims, for we lose our fathers and brothers."

Realizing the wisdom of the women's appeal, the Sabines called off the attack, made peace with the Romans, and agreed to become allies.

According to the stories, Romulus ruled wisely for the rest of his reign but carried on intermittent wars, for example, with the Etruscan city of Veii, located ten miles (16km) north of Rome on the Cremera River, a tributary of the Tiber. It is said that he selected one hundred of the wisest men from the noblest families to form the Senate, which was to function as a special advisory body to him. The legends proclaim that after a long and successful rule, while reviewing his troops one day, Romulus was covered by a cloud and taken directly to heaven, where he was transformed into the god Quirinus, who presided over war and weapons.

Rome Under the Monarchy

NUMA POMPILIUS

Numa Pompilius, whose legendary dates of rule were from 715 to 673 B.C., was reportedly the next Roman king. He was a Sabine, and some of the best Roman families of the later Republic claimed descent from him. Livy records that the Roman people elected him to cement their relations with the Sabines. His reign was remembered as a time of peace. Supposedly he met every night with the goddess Egeria in a tiny cave just outside the Capenan Gate to the city, where she instructed him on the correct way to worship the gods and predict the future by reading cattle livers and entrails. This knowledge allowed him to reform the Roman religion and also bring about changes in the structure of the Roman government. He built a number of temples, created the institution of the Vestal Virgins (the guardians of the Temple of the goddess Vesta, in which the sacred flame of the city burned), and established the first formal calendar. In addition, Numa instituted the custom of electing a king instead of recognizing a hereditary succession. Once elected, however, the Roman kings had nearly absolute power (although custom dictated that they consult with the Senate). Their actions, Numa declared, were subject only to approval of the *Comitia Curiata*, a popular assembly made up of free citizens.

TULLUS HOSTILIUS

The forty-two years of peace under Numa Pompilius stand in contrast to the eras of both his predecessor and his successor. When the third king of Rome, Tullus Hostilius, was elected — his legendary dates of reign are from 673 to 641 B.C. — Rome found itself at war with many of the people in the immediate area.

The chief enemies of Rome at this time were the Albans to the south, the descendants of the inhabitants of Alba Longa, and the Etruscans to the north, who lived in Veii and Fidenae, the same two cities that had troubled Romulus. War between the Albans and

Below: A sinuous Etruscan figurine depicts a mermaid. Until the first half of the third century B.C., Roman art was dominated by the Etruscans, who taught the Romans to sculpt in bronze and construct temples and public buildings. By about 250 B.C., however, the Romans had begun to turn to the Greeks for artistic and architectural inspiration.

Rome Under the Monarchy

Romans consisted of a series of cattle raids back and forth across the frontier. The two sides finally settled the matter in one pitched battle at a spot halfway between Rome and Alba Longa. Unfortunately, the Etruscans decided to intervene; they mobilized their army and marched to the site.

The appearance of the Etruscans caused King Tullus Hostilius to call a truce with the Albans and to request a meeting with their king, Mettius Fufetius. Tullus' concern was that if the Romans and Albans fought, the winner, whomever that might be, would be

so weakened that the Etruscan army could fall upon them and defeat them with little effort. Rather than let this happen, Tullus proposed that the Albans and Romans each choose three champions; the six men would then fight it out, with victory going to whichever side's champions won. In this manner, the Romans assured that their army would be able to maintain close to full strength for the expected battle with the Etrsucans should the Roman warriors beat the Albans.

Tullus Hostilius selected triplets from the family of the Horatii, and Mettius Fufetius found a set of

Rome Under the Monarchy

triplets among the family of the Curiatii. The duel commenced, and to the horror of the Roman onlookers, two of the Horatii were quickly killed, while the Curiatii survived; one was wounded badly, another slightly, and a third had no wound at all. The unwounded Horatius turned and fled rather than face the combined threat of all three Albans. Yet his flight was not without a plan. As the three Curiatii pursued him, the wounds of the two slowed them down until they both staggered along well behind their unwounded brother. Having separated the three, the Roman turned quickly, surprised the Alban, who could not check his headlong run, and killed him. The Roman then ran back and easily dispatched the two wounded Curiatii, whose injuries had caused them to tire quickly during the chase. The Etruscans, seeing their opportunity gone, returned to their cities.

The surviving Horatius returned to a hero's welcome in Rome. As he entered the city, however, he saw his own sister weeping. Thinking it strange that his sister should cry at his moment of glory, he asked her the reason. When he learned that one of the Curiatii triplets had been her betrothed, he drew his sword and struck off his own sister's head, exclaiming,

"Thus should it be to those who weep for the enemies of Rome!" The crowd was shocked, for the brother had violated a basic Roman law—only a father had an unlimited right to kill his own children. This created a dilemma: the penalty for killing a sibling was death, but the man who, according to the law, deserved that penalty had been the salvation of the city. The soldier was seized, bound, and tried, with the judges regretfully decreeing death. The young soldier's father appealed to the judges, saying that had his son not killed the girl, he would have; his appeal saved his son's life. However, many Romans disagreed with the outcome, feeling that such liberal interpretations of the law could lead to weakness in the state.

Unpleasant as this aftermath had been, the overall result was good, for the Albans abandoned the city of Alba Longa and moved to Rome, where they settled on the Caelian, south of the settlement on the Palatine. By and large they proved good allies. Only once, during a battle with the Etruscans from Fidenae, did the Romans have reason to doubt the Albans' loyalty. In that battle, Mettius Fufetius arrived late on the battlefield and held his troops back

Rome Under the Monarchy

ANCUS MARCIUS

Wars against the other inhabitants of Latium continued under Ancus Marcius (r. 641–617 B.C.), the next king. Legends tell how he conquered the nearby cities of Politorium, Tennenae, Ficana, and Medullia and forcefully relocated their populations to Rome, where Roman citizenship was conferred upon them and they were made to settle on the Aventine and on the Janiculum, a hill across the Tiber from the other seven hills.

Livy credited Ancus Marcius with creating the office of Pontifex Maximus, whose chief duty was to manage the city's religious calendar and ensure that all ceremonies were performed according to the correct rituals. An intriguing legendary event associated with Ancus Marcius is his construction of the first bridge across the Tiber. While no evidence substantiates the building of a bridge at this time, it is interesting that the term Pontifex Maximus means "Great Bridge Builder." The island in the middle of the Tiber made the site of Rome the perfect place to bridge the river. Also, two trails began at the mouth of the Tiber, \ran on separate sides through the salt marshes, and converged on Rome. Joining these two trails with a bridge must have been an economic boon for the city.

Above: The Tomb of the Leopards (c. 475 B.C.) near Tarquinia features wall paintings of a riotous party complete with dancing and drinking to the tune of flutes, castanets, and lyres, such as the one this Etruscan musician holds.

from the fighting to see who would win, reasoning that by hesitating he would guarantee fighting on the winning side. However, the Romans saw his treachery and, after winning the battle, seized him, bound him between two chariots facing opposite directions, and whipped the horses into full gallop so that he was ripped in two: "Just as yesterday you could not decide which direction to follow, either Fidenae or Rome, so today we spare you the mental agony of such indecision." The sight of Mettius Fufetius' torn corpse so disgusted the Romans that they swore from then on to use only humane methods of execution.

LUCIUS TARQUINIUS PRISCUS AND THE ETRUSCANS

The ascendancy of Lucius Tarquinius Priscus (r. 617–579 B.C.), the next king, gives historians a clue about the growing influence of the Etruscans on the evolution of early Rome. The Etruscans had been an important presence in Italy since at least 1000 B.C. Their legacy is a series of mysteries: they wrote using a Greek alphabet but their language, which is still being deciphered, is not Greek; some archaeological evidence suggests that they migrated to Italy from the eastern end of the Mediterranean, yet other indicators seem to show they were indigenous to Italy; some signs indicate that they conquered Rome militarily at the end of the seventh century B.C., but other evidence suggests that they never conquered Rome but were simply assimilated by the Romans.

By about 670 B.C., the Etruscans, living north of Rome in what is now Tuscany, were trading with the Greeks who came to Etruria (as historians call the homeland of the Etruscans) in search of the iron ore that the Etruscans mined in abundance. In exchange, the Greeks proffered their culture, art, alphabet, religion, and military and governmental skills, and by 600 B.C. the Etruscans had adopted a great deal of Greek culture, which in turn would become part of the evolving Roman culture.

By that time the king of Rome was Lucius Tarquinius Priscus, the first Etruscan king. Livy and other ancient historians maintained that he was not a conqueror but was merely elected to the position. Livy writes that Tarquinius, from a noble family in the city of Tarquinia, immigrated to Rome in search of opportunity—he and his wife, Tanaquil, gathered up their wealth and traveled there by wagon. At the end of their journey, just before they entered Rome, they stopped at the top of the Janiculum, across the Tiber from Rome, to look out over the city. At that point, an eagle suddenly swooped down and snatched the hat from Tarquinius' head, flew high in the sky, and then swooped back down to place the hat back on his head. Tanaquil took this as an omen:

the eagle, the symbol of Rome, had symbolically placed a crown on her husband's head. He would someday rule the city.

Tarquinius bought a house in Rome and used his considerable wealth and outgoing personality to become an important man-about-town. His wealth and winning personality made him popular, and he became a trusted advisor to King Ancus Marcius. Upon the king's death, the people of Rome elected Tarquinius as his successor. Whether this legend records an actual series of events or whether the Romans later created this myth about a peaceful takeover by the Etruscans in order to conceal from posterity an actual military conquest of Rome has been an actively

25

debated question among historians. What is certain, however, is that there was a significant infusion of Etruscan culture into Rome at this time.

The legends about the reign of Lucius Tarquinius Priscus certainly suggest that it was from the Etruscans that the Romans learned to build cities, temples, and fortifications. According to Livy, Tarquinius built the first fortress on top of the Capitoline, along with the Temple of Jupiter, Juno, and Minerva, and he began to drain and pave over the marsh at the base of the Capitoline and Palatine hills.

SERVIUS TULLIUS

Servius Tullius (r. 579–534 B.C.) rose from slavery to become king of Rome. Livy recounted that Servius was originally one of Tarquinius' slaves. One day, Tanaquil, Tarquinius' wife, looked out of her window into the palace courtyard and saw Servius sleeping on a bench. Suddenly the boy's bright red hair burst into flame. Tanaquil ran downstairs and doused the boy's head with a bucket of water, at which point the child woke up. Tanaquil was amazed to learn that his hair frequently burst into flame yet never caused the slightest damage to his head. Intrigued by this phenomenon, Tanaquil made the boy a personal attendant to herself and Tarquinius. Servius quickly showed himself to be so intelligent and capable that the king, ignoring his own sons, Arruns and Tarquinius, encouraged Servius as his successor by allowing the boy to marry his own daughter.

Servius was remarkably personable, and the Romans regarded him well. When Tarquinius was assassinated several years later, Servius had no trouble skillfully maneuvering himself into being elected king, and once in power he continued Tarquinius' reforms for Rome. First, he completely reorganized the Roman army. He began by outfitting the soldiers with Greek armor and weapons; he also devised a new tactical formation of troops packed tightly into a rectangle three to seven lines deep, called the phalanx, which gave the Romans a military edge over their neighbors. Next he reorganized the government, creating a new popular assembly called the *Comitia Centuriata*, whose function was to act as an advisory council for the king and Senate, along with the Comitia Curiata. By giving the people a voice in government, Servius enlisted their support.

Servius expanded the boundaries of Rome to include the Quirinal and Viminal hills. He built the Temple to Diana on the Aventine. Probably because he had been a slave as a boy, he is said to have allowed slaves to become citizens after they had gained their freedom (any free person who lived in the city of Rome automatically became a citizen). Legend also credits him with building the famous Servian Wall, the first wall to surround the whole city.

According to legend, Servius was assassinated at the instigation of his own daughter, Tullia, and her husband, Tarquinius, the son of Lucius Tarquinius Priscus. Sometime after he had become king, Servius Tullius had married his two daughters, Tullia I and Tullia II, to his predecessor's sons, Arruns and Tarquinius, respectively. (The Romans did not formally name their daughters. If the young woman was not known by a family nickname, she was addressed with a feminized form of the family name. If there was more than one daughter, each simply received a number.)

According to legend, Tullia I was, from childhood, a vicious, scheming girl who hated her father, while her sister, Tullia II, was gentle and loving. Tullia I married Arruns, who was as gentle and pleasant as his wife was villainous and unpleasant. Tullia II married Tarquinius, who had a personality that delighted in cruel jokes and contorted intrigue. It was not long before Tullia I and Tarquinius realized that they were made for each other. Tullia I murdered her good-natured spouse; Tarquinius murdered his. After a suitable period of mourning, the two came together, married, and turned their equally warped minds to the task of plotting the murder of Servius Tullius.

One day, Tarquinius entered the building where the Senate met. He boldly seated himself in the king's chair and began to rant and rave against Servius Tullius. When Servius entered the building, Tarquinius seized the old man, beat him up, and threw him outside, where two assassins were waiting to kill him. While Servius' body lay bleeding in the street, Tullia I approached in her chariot. She drove the horses and chariot over the body of her father so fast that his spurting blood covered the chariot and her clothing.

In this gruesome state, she hurried home to her husband to plot their next move. Immediately, Tarquinius—who became known as Tarquinius Superbus— declared himself king without any pretense of an election and instituted a brutal dictatorship over the stunned city.

TARQUINIUS SUPERBUS

The reign of Tarquinius Superbus (the Proud) from 534 to 509 B.C. was legendary as the worst in Roman history. He certainly began badly by refusing an honorable burial for the murdered Servius. He executed several members of the Senate who had been especially close to the murdered king. He appointed mercenaries to protect him from the vengeance of an angry people and used this guard to murder anyone he even suspected of treachery and to confiscate their property for himself.

Tarquinius also engaged in a number of generally successful wars against neighboring cities of Latium. With the loot from these conquests, he began a massive construction program in Rome that included building the Temple of Jupiter on the Capitoline, enlarging the amphitheater, and expanding the *Cloaca Maxima*, the canal that drained the Forum. He forced some of the people of the lower classes to work on the Cloaca Maxima, which, since it also served as the city sewer, was an especially menial job, fit only for slaves.

THE REVOLT AGAINST TARQUINIUS

Tarquinius thus succeeded in alienating both the upper and lower classes. Yet his bodyguards prevented an open rebellion until his rule became so oppressive that the entire population rebelled.

With the people against him, Tarquinius and his family retreated to the Etruscan town of Caere, north of Rome, but he intended to return. His plot to come back to Rome began with a visit to Lars Porsena, the king of Clusium (modern-day Chiusi). Lars Porsena, along with Tarquinius Superbus and his son Sextus, organized an army and led it back to Rome.

As dramatic as the tales of rebels Lucretia, Horatius Cocles, and Gaius Mucius are (see sidebar on page 30), they are probably legendary—though, as in all revolts, feats of heroism certainly occurred. Cornelius Tacitus (A.D. 56–c. 118), one of ancient Rome's most famous historians, recorded that Porsena won the battle, forced the surrender of the city, and may even have ruled in Rome for a few years until some of the Latin tribes attacked and defeated him. This is the kind of disgrace that later Romans would have liked to ignore, and perhaps these stories were made up to soothe painful memories.

THE END OF THE KINGS

In any event, within a few years, by some means that historians are not completely clear about, the Romans had rid themselves of the Etruscan

kings. Once they were gone, the Romans were determined never to suffer the rule of a tyrant again, and they created a new form of government—one that preserved some of the political powers of a king but removed the possibility of dictatorship. In this new organization, Rome would be ruled by two consuls, each elected to a single one-year term by the *Comitia*

Centuriata; the idea was that the consuls could check each other's power. Roman tradition established 509 B.C. as the year the first two consuls, Lucius Junius Brutus and Lucius Tarquinius Collatinus, the same Collatinus whose wife was raped by Sextus (see sidebar on page 31), were appointed and the Roman Republic was founded.

see sidebar on page 30; see sidebar on page 31

Above: While Roman history has its share of evil, immoral, and scheming women, the ideal hearkened back to women like Lucretia, who always placed children, husband, and nation above themselves.

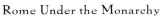

Rome Under the Monarchy

Three Heroes

Horatius Cocles

As the Etruscan army of Tarquinius Superbus, Sextus, and Lars Porsena approached the Janiculum to retake the city, hundreds of frightened Romans poured across the Tiber Bridge into Rome. One Roman, Horatius Cocles (the One-Eyed), tried to rally them to defend the west end of the bridge and thus the city itself. Only two of his friends agreed to stand with him, although Horatius managed to get some people to start tearing down the bridge behind him.

For a short time, the three held the bridge against all comers while Romans behind them furiously chopped at the bridge supports. Stunned by this brave defense, the Etruscans drew back. When the bridge behind them was nearly down, Horatius persuaded his friends to retreat and he held the bridge alone, gaining precious minutes by challenging the various leaders of the Etruscans to single combat. None of them took up his provocation, but the Etruscan mass surged forward against the lone hero. At that moment, according to Livy, the eastern end of the bridge crashed into the Tiber and Horatius stood isolated on the western end. According to legend, he cast off a prayer to the god Tiber and threw himself in full armor into the river, where Tiber, impressed by his courage, buoyed him up until he reached the other side.

Gaius Mucius

Gallant as the example of Horatius Cocles had been, Lars Porsena managed to surround the city and settle into a long siege. Food soon grew scarce, and just when it looked as if Rome would have to surrender, a young nobleman, Gaius Mucius, decided to cross the Tiber, assassinate Lars Porsena, and save the city. (In this ancient period, if the king died, an army generally gave up the campaign.) When Gaius approached Porsena's tent, however, he realized, somewhat belatedly, that he did not know what Porsena looked like. He saw two men sitting outside the royal tent at a table covered with food, and rather than give up his desperate venture, the young man stepped forward, picked one of the men, and jammed a dagger into his heart. Unfortunately, he killed Porsena's secretary. Immediately he was seized and condemned by an angry Porsena to be burned alive.

Faced with certain death, Gaius Mucius tried a last gamble. He laughed at the sentence and announced that the Romans held such a punishment in contempt. To illustrate that contempt, he thrust his right hand into the flame on a nearby altar and stood impassively, not making a sound nor changing facial expression as the fire burned his hand off! The Etruscans watched this display in amazement. Finally Gaius Mucius withdrew a blackened stump from the fire, pointed it at Porsena, and lied: "There are three hundred other young Romans of equal courage waiting in the city to assassinate you. They will come, one at a time, until one finally kills you." Lars Porsena was stunned. He had no desire to face three hundred such heroes and offered to release Gaius, make peace with Rome, and take his army back home. Gaius Mucius returned to Rome in triumph, and the Senate awarded him a grant of farmland and the cognomen *Scaevola*, meaning "Lefty," to add to his name.

Lucretia

The revolt that brought down the tyrant Tarquinius Superbus was due not directly to his harsh and arbitrary rule, but to the disgraceful behavior of his son Tarquinius Sextus, an excessively arrogant and duplicitous youth. One evening, while the Roman army was besieging Ardea, a Latin city south of Rome, Tarquinius Sextus and his cousin, Lucius Tarquinius Collatinus, were drinking. As the evening wore on, the conversation went to the subject of wives, and an argument began over who had the most virtuous wife. As the argument progressed and the wine flowed, Collatinus proposed that they ride quickly back to their homes, surprise their wives, and see which one was engaged in the most honorable and wifely activity. When they arrived at Sextus' domicile, his wife was in the midst of a riotous dinner party, but they found Collatinus' wife, Lucretia, engaged in spinning.

The sight of Lucretia's earnest spinning while his own wife ate and drank created a perverse passion in Sextus to seduce Lucretia. Several days later he returned to Rome and tried his best to tempt her with sweet words. When she refused him, Sextus threatened to rape her, kill her, then murder a slave and place the body next to hers. He would then tell Collatinus that he had discovered the two making love and killed both of them. Poor Lucretia, realizing the hopelessness of her situation, submitted. After Sextus had left, however, Lucretia sent messages to her husband and father asking them to hurry home. When they arrived, she told them her story and demanded that they avenge the insult. Then, before they could

stop her, she took a dagger from within the folds of her skirt and drove it into her heart, exclaiming, as she lay dying, that in killing herself she removed the temptation of future Roman wives who might cry rape to disguise a sexual liaison. Collatinus carried his wife's body to the Forum, where he recounted the sad, heroic tale to the Roman populace. With one mind, they rose against Tarquinius and drove him from the throne.

The focal point of this wall decoration in the Tomb of the Lionesses (c. 510 B.C.) near the Etruscan city of Tarquinia seems to be the giant krater between the two men directly above the opening. Kraters were used to mix wine and water, since the ancients did not drink undiluted wine. The figures on each side of the men are dancing.

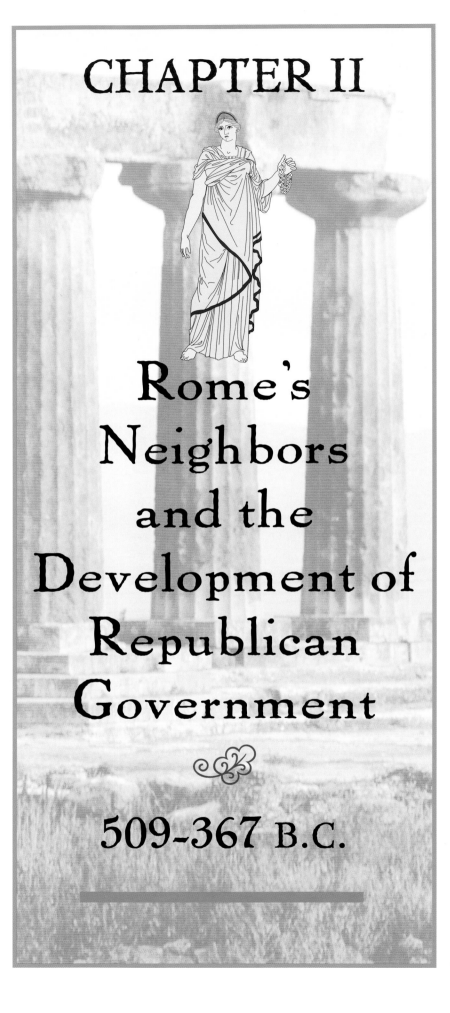

CHAPTER II

Rome's Neighbors and the Development of Republican Government

509-367 B.C.

LIVY GAVE US AN INSTRUCtive scene from the early days of the Republic— one that reveals not only the chronic warfare with foreigners that troubled Rome at this time, but the political and economic pressures that resulted from this violent period.

In 495 B.C., an old, ragged, emaciated man appeared in the Roman Forum. People were put off by his appearance until somebody recognized him as an old plebeian (plebeians were members of the lower class, distinct from patricians, members of the upper class) soldier who had served valiantly in the wars against the Sabines. People pointed out that he had even been the commander of a century, a troop of one hundred soldiers. Once they knew him, they gathered around, curious about how such a valiant and venerable soldier could have come to such a miserable state. His explanation excited the sympathy of all the listeners. As a soldier in the legions he was required to serve far afield; consequently, he was unable to prevent Sabine raiders from destroying his crops and burning his home. When he returned after the war, he needed money to pay back taxes and to rebuild his farm. He borrowed the money, but a poor crop prevented his paying back the loan, so his creditors seized him and sold him into slavery to pay the debt. The people who heard this story knew that all of this was perfectly legal, but it offended their sensibilities, especially when the old fellow showed them the bruises and welts on his body that had been raised by a beating from his master—a Roman like himself.

The story caused a general tumult, which in turn brought a larger number of people out, including many other debt slaves, all from the plebeian class. Thoroughly incensed, the people brought the abused man before the two patrician consuls of that year, Publius Servilius and Appius Claudius. The crowd demanded that the consuls find redress for the old soldier's wrongs. At first neither consul wanted to suggest a solution, but in the midst of the stalemate, a messenger brought word that a Volscan army was approaching the city. Immediately, the consuls ordered the population in the Forum to disperse, secure their war gear, and reassemble in their legions to defend the city.

To the patricians' astonishment, the people refused to act until the consuls had dealt with the grievance at hand. After all, taking up their swords to defend their country could land them in the same situation as the debt slaves. They asked, "What was the difference between being a slave to a Volscan or a Roman?" The consensus among the plebeians was to let the patricians fight alone. When the Volsci came within sight of the gates, Publius Servilius, the more reasonable of the two consuls, issued an edict on the spot that henceforth it would be illegal to chain or beat a Roman citizen in such a way that it would keep him from his military duties. Furthermore, it would be illegal to sell or impound the property of any soldier who had fallen into debt because of army service.

Unfortunately, Livy fabricated this happy ending. Debt slavery was not abolished during Servilius' consulship, and the practice continued for another fifty years. Livy's story, however, illustrates two real problems that the early Republic faced: foreign invaders who targeted Rome and social and economic problems that threatened the state from within. Dealing with

Rome's Neighbors and the Development of
Republican Government

foreign invaders and coping with these social and economic problems would consume Rome's creative energy for the next two and a half centuries.

ROME'S STRUGGLE FOR CENTRAL ITALY

The years before and after 509 B.C. are, tradition holds, the years when the Etruscan nobility left Rome, taking with them the protection of the Etruscan military power. From then on, Rome would have to stand on her own against numerous local tribes that wanted the easy Tiber River crossing, the salt sources at the mouth of the Tiber, and the rich grazing lands on the slopes of the seven hills. The Roman army would have many opportunities to use its new tactic, the phalanx formation, in defense of this coveted city and its surroundings. (Rome itself controlled an area only about ten miles [16km] in diameter out from the city itself.)

First among Rome's enemies at this time were the tribes of Latium. The Latins were linguistically and culturally kin to the Romans, but they owed allegiance to different city-states. Around the year 500 B.C., eight of the Latin towns formed the Latin League, which fought not only assorted hill tribes but also Rome itself. In 499 B.C., the Romans soundly defeated the league in a battle at Lake Regillus, ten miles (16km) southeast of Rome. Soon afterward, the league signed a treaty of alliance, called the Foedus Cassium (named for Spurius Cassius Vecellinus, a man who attended the treaty signing), with the Romans.

THE VOLSCI

With a truce between the Latin League and the Romans enacted, the new allies found themselves subject to attacks from non-Latin tribes: the Volsci, Aequi, Sabines, and the Etruscans of Veii, a city north of Rome. By the 490s, the Volsci, originally from the Apennines, had extended their territory into southern Latium and westward to the coast, where they seized the previously Roman-held town of Antium (modern Anzio). Using Antium as a base, the Volsci began raiding north toward Rome, and several times they came within sight of the city itself.

In 491 B.C., according to Livy, a Volscan army led by a renegade Roman patrician named Gaius Marcius Cariolanus nearly took Rome and was only prevented from doing so by Gaius' mother, who persuaded him to spare the city of his birth. The Volsci, however, would remain a serious threat for nearly two centuries. In 338 B.C., the Roman consul Gaius Maenius defeated the Volsci's fleet. He took the bronze rams called the *rostra* off their warships and decorated the base of the speaker's platform in the Roman Forum with them to commemorate his victory. The Volsci were not decisively defeated, though, and as late as 304 B.C., they joined the Samnites, another Apennine tribe, in a war against Rome.

THE AEQUI

At the same time that they were fighting the Volsci, the Romans also had to contend with the Aequi, who threatened Rome from the east. The Aequi were another Apennine tribe; they lived just east of the Latin towns of Tibur and Praeneste. In 458 B.C., the Aequi trapped the consul Lucinius Minucius and the Roman army he was leading on Mount Aligidus. The situation moved the Roman Senate to beg the famous ex-consul Lucius Quinctius Cincinnatus to leave his plow, assume the dictatorship—that is, absolute power granted by the Senate in a state of emergency—and destroy the Aequian army. While Cincinnatus' heroic action did save Minucius' army, the Aequi were not decisively beaten, and they remained a military threat until 304 B.C., when Rome nearly exterminated them.

THE SABINES

During this same period, a third group of mountain dwellers, the Sabines, also threatened Rome periodically. The Sabines, who inhabited areas north of the Aequi, had been an irritation to the Romans since the legendary days of Romulus after the abduction of the Sabine women. While some of the Sabines identified themselves with the Romans, others remained bitter enemies throughout the period of the Roman kingdom and well into the Republic period. These Sabines often allied themselves with the Volsci and Aequi, and troubled the Romans chiefly as guerrilla warriors who attacked isolated Roman farms and villages. In 494 B.C., the Roman dictator Manlius Valerius inflicted a major defeat on an army of Volsci and Sabines near Velitrae (modern Velletri), twenty miles (32km) southeast of Rome, but these tribes continued to harass Roman territory periodically until 290 B.C., when the consul Marcus Curius Dentatus decisively defeated them. Livy called the Sabines, masters of the lightning raid, "Rome's most dangerous enemies."

Left: A marble relief from the side of a sarcophagus of the third century A.D. portrays the Greek hero Oedipus sacrificing to the Delphic Oracle. The oracle at Delphi was the most famous oracle in the ancient world, and even the early Roman Republic sent delegations there to ask the guidance of the gods.

VEII

Unhappily for Rome, the Volsci, Aequi, and Sabines were not the only enemies in the neighborhood. Ten miles (16km) north of Rome lay the strategic Etruscan city of Veii, a town that laid claim to land directly across the Tiber River from Rome. Veii and Rome were natural enemies, since both wanted to control the economically important crossing of the Tiber at Tiber Island and the salt flats at the mouth of that river.

Veii and Rome had sporadically raided each other since the expulsion of Tarquinius Superbus. In 482 B.C., however, the Aequi and the Veientes simultaneously launched an invasion into Roman territory, marking the beginning of a long, brutal war. This was potentially the most serious threat to Rome, since the Veientes' army was also trained in the phalanx formation. In 477 B.C., the Romans lost an entire army at the Battle of the Cremera River, forcing them to negotiate a temporary peace with Veii. Within a few years, however, both cities were sending raiding parties into each others' territories, and in 426, regular, large-scale warfare had broken out again. This time, the Romans seized Fidenae, an Etruscan city allied with Veii. In 405, Roman armies laid siege to Veii itself.

Livy—who might have been trying to excite Roman patriotic sentiments by comparing this siege to that of Troy—claims this siege lasted until 396, a full ten years. Like the Greeks at Troy, the Romans took Veii by an elaborate trick. Instead of hiding in a Trojan horse, they excavated a tunnel under the walls of Veii, and while some Roman troops launched an assault against the walls, a select force of Rome's best soldiers broke out of the tunnel in the middle of Veii to attack the defenders from behind. Marcus Furius Camillus, the Roman consul in command, ordered a general massacre of the men and sold the women and children into slavery. The loot from Veii was immense; the Romans sent one-tenth of it as a thanksgiving offering to the shrine of the god Apollo at Delphi in Greece. The larger and more sophisticated Greek cities periodically sent victory offerings of this sort to Delphi as a kind of religious boast. Rome may have been making her own symbolic gesture that she was now a player on the international scene, and in fact, by 396, Rome controlled a territory many times larger than most Greek city-states.

THE CELTIC MENACE

Just when it seemed that Rome had achieved some stability in central Italy, there emerged a new menace: the Celts, a people who had lived in central Europe since at least 1500 B.C. and who shared their Indo-European ancestry with the Romans. By the fourth century, however, neither the Celts nor the Romans realized any familial affinity—to the Romans, as to the Greeks before them, the Celts were simply savage and fearsome barbarians. The Celts were attracted to the warm climate of Italy and regarded the Romans as mere obstacles to be swept aside. Livy claims that the Gauls—the Celts from what is today France—came to Italy for the wine, because their colder homeland north of the Alps could not produce grapes.

Whatever the invaders' motivations, the Gauls were in northern Italy around 450 B.C. By 387 B.C., they had subjugated most of the Etruscan towns north of Rome and had laid siege to Clusium. When the people of Clusium asked Rome for aid, the Romans sent ambassadors to meet with the Gauls. Unfortunately, one of the Romans, Quintus Fabius, lost his temper and killed the Gauls' chief. He returned to Rome, and the Gauls demanded that the Romans turn him over for punishment; when the Senate refused, the Gauls marched on Rome.

In response, the Romans appointed the hotheaded Quintus Fabius general of the army. When he led the army to meet the Gauls at the mouth of the Allia River, however, he lost control of his men, who panicked and retreated as a mob back to Rome. According to Livy, their terror was such that the retreating soldiers did

The Men of Rome

Since there was neither enough room nor enough food in the Capitoline fortress for the entire population of Rome, the Senate decided that the old and infirm would be sent into the countryside in the hopes that the Gauls would spare them. Some of the oldest senators refused to leave, choosing instead to sit calmly in front of their homes, dressed in their best robes, to await death with dignity. The Gauls approached the open and deserted city cautiously, fearing a trap. According to legend; the old senators sat so still that the Gauls took them for statues until one of the barbarians reached out and tugged at the beard of Marcus Papirius—who promptly hit him on the head with his short ivory senatorial staff. The enraged Gaul killed Papirius, and a general slaughter of the defenseless old men began while their homes and the public buildings of Rome were looted and burned.

not even pause to close the gates of Rome as they rushed to take refuge in the fortress at the top of the Capitoline.

The Gauls stayed for seven months, making two attempts to take the Capitoline. The Roman defenders met the first assault head on and repelled the Gauls. The second attack was foiled by what the Romans felt was divine intervention. When the Gauls tried to creep up the slopes of the Capitoline at night, the sleeping Romans were awakened by the cackling of Juno's sacred geese, which lived within the precincts of her temple and which even in their hunger the Romans had not eaten out of reverence for the goddess. The Romans believed that the animals' warning represented her gratitude. In any event, the Gauls did not attack again.

Meanwhile, in the countryside, Marcus Furius Camillus, the victor at Veii, tried to organize the Romans outside the walls into a relief army. The strength of the Roman fortifications coupled with the threat of a Roman army behind them prompted the Gauls to accept a ransom of one thousand pounds of gold for withdrawing from the city. When the Roman negotiator, Quintus Sulpicius, objected to the Gallic chieftain, Brennus, that his scales were dishonest, Brennus threw his sword onto the scale and uttered *"Vae victis"* — "Woe to the vanquished." The Romans, realizing the hopelessness of the situation, paid the ransom.

The patriotic Livy wanted his readers to believe that a relief army arrived, forced the Gauls to leave without the ransom, then pursued and destroyed the invaders. However, no other ancient source mentions this timely, if contrived, intervention. Instead, the Romans seem to have paid the ransom and even, for a time, contemplated abandoning their ruined city and migrating en masse to Veii. To abandon the temples that bound the people to Rome, however, would have been a sacrilege.

THE PLIGHT OF THE CITIZEN-SOLDIERS

During these hard years of almost constant warfare, cracks had begun to appear in Roman society that threatened to tear it apart. Livy's story about the ex-soldier held as a slave dramatizes these internal problems, and this old man, a representative of the plebeian class, was not alone in his dilemma.

Between 509 and 400 B.C., Rome was continually at war. Yet the city had no standing army, and this was at the root of the problems of the plebeian class, which provided soldiers as the need arose. The bulk of the Roman army was made up of infantrymen who supplied their own weapons and armor according to their economic ability, estimated on the basis of how much property they owned. It was a tidy military system with one flaw—should a campaign last too long, those soldiers who were also farmers faced economic hardships and even bankruptcy.

Roman agriculture required intensive effort to plant, harvest, and process crops. The Romans' staple grain—far, or spelt—has such a heavy, tough husk that threshing and winnowing it to separate the kernel was a laborious endeavor. It was a lucky farmer, and probably one blessed with numerous sons, who could produce enough food to survive an unusually long military campaign. As the Roman army spent more and more time campaigning, a growing number of soldiers returned home to find their families either hungry or forced to survive on next year's seed crop.

To bridge the period of scarcity, Roman farmers turned to moneylenders, who financed the farmers until the next crop could be sold. These loans were secured on the body of the debtor, and the law gave a creditor the right to seize a debtor, put him in chains, and sell him to recover his debt. The law even stipulated that

in the event no buyer could be found to purchase the man, his multiple creditors could divide him up. While some historians have assumed this meant physically cutting the debtor into pieces, it more probably meant dividing his property between his creditors.

A PEACEFUL REVOLUTION

It is not surprising that hardworking farmers who had fallen into debt as a result of their service to their country would demand a remedy. In 494 B.C., the plebeians collectively refused to fight in the army, physically withdrawing from the area around the Palatine and Capitoline hills and occupying the Aventine. There, they formed their own government led by two (which increased over the years to ten) elected officials known as tribunes, who presided over an exclusively plebeian assembly called the *Concilium Plebis Tributa*. Besides leading the plebeians before the

consuls and assembly, the tribunes also acted as spokesmen for the welfare of both individual plebeians and their class. These tribunes were assisted by two elected aediles, who guarded the plebeian treasury and archives in the Temples of Ceres, Liber, and Libera on the Aventine. The plebeians bound themselves by a sacred oath, the *Lex Sacrata*, to protect the tribunes and aediles with their lives.

At first this plebeian government—made up of the Concilium Plebis Tributa, the tribunes, and the aediles—had no standing under Roman law, and certainly the patricians would have liked to ignore it. Yet the new organization derived a considerable amount of power from the fact that as an organized political body, the plebeians could withhold military service whenever the tribunes saw an opportunity to gain a political advantage. The patricians had to consider this a serious threat since they were too few to protect Roman Latium alone. As a result, the patricians began grudgingly to grant concessions. Five times between 494 and

287 B.C., the plebeians would threaten to refuse military service, thereby gradually gaining enough rights to establish what was in effect another branch of government, associated with but as yet politically separate from the older patrician government.

The Roman government thus evolved into two bodies. The patricians led one with two consuls and the Senate, which dictated policy to the comparatively weak popular assembly, the Comitia Centuriata; the other branch, the Concilium Plebis Tributa, led by tribunes, represented the will of the plebeians.

For a group of people whose power was considerable, the plebeians' demands were very conservative. Rather than sweeping changes that would radically alter the government, they proposed reforms of the existing political and economic order. For instance, about 456 B.C., the patrician-dominated Comitia Centuriata approved the *Lex Ililia*, giving the plebeians title to a specific area on the Aventine, and in 454 B.C., the same assembly passed the *Lex Aternia-Tarpeia*, a law preventing a consul from imposing any fine equal to more than the value of thirty oxen and two sheep.

THE TWELVE TABLETS

In 451 B.C., the plebeians achieved one of their most significant concessions from the patricians when they had the patricians commit the body of Roman law to writing. This document, known as the Twelve Tablets, guaranteed more consistency when applying the law than reliance upon oral tradition and the goodwill of the patrician consuls who acted as judges.

The Twelve Tablets became the cornerstone of Roman law, and thus of a number of subsequent legal codes, into our own times. Originally inscribed on wooden (some sources say bronze) tablets, they were set up in the Roman Forum, where the early consuls held their legal sessions. The tablets were not a compilation of all Roman laws, but a summary of specific laws that the plebeians felt patrician consuls might interpret against the interests of plebeian litigants. The first three tablets dealt with trial procedure, including the conditions under which a defendant might be compelled to come into court, the amount of bond a consul could levy on an accused person, how and where a consul's decision should be published, and the proper length of a trial.

Tablet Three also dealt with the issue of Roman citizens becoming slaves—the very subject that had initiated the plebeian uprising. The laws on this tablet, though not abolishing debt slavery, assured the rights of the debtor. A creditor could still seize a debtor, even

if he was a soldier, and put him in chains, but those chains could not weigh more than fifteen pounds (7kg) and the creditor was ordered to feed his prisoner at least a pound (454g) of grain a day. The debtor had a fixed number of days to raise the amount he owed, but at the end of sixty days the creditor could bring his captive into the court and on three successive days announce the amount of the debt. If nobody came forward to pay the amount, the creditor could kill the debtor or sell him across the Tiber as a slave. Enslavement for debt remained a part of Roman law until 326 B.C., when the plebeians were able to force the Senate to recommend abolition of the practice to the Comitia Centuriata.

Tablets Four through Seven dealt with family, wills, ownership, and inheritance. The laws stated that the father's wishes were paramount: he could kill a deformed child of his at birth and exercised complete control over his daughters until they married, whereupon they became the legal property of their husbands. Tablet Five, among other things, permitted the state to appoint a guardian to administer the estate of a person who was insane or exhibited spendthrift behavior.

Tablet Eight dealt with slander and torts, and gives us an insight into the cruelty of ancient Roman law. Anyone who composed an insulting song about a person could be beaten to death; anyone who stole crops at night from another was to be hanged in the Temple of Ceres, goddess of agriculture, as a sacrifice; and anyone who burned down a house or a pile of his neighbor's wheat was to be burned at the stake. If somebody cut down his neighbor's tree during the day, the fine was 25 *asses* (an *as* was a designated weight in copper—Rome would have no coinage for another 180 years), but if he did it at night, the tree's owner could kill him with impunity.

Tablets Nine through Twelve dealt with specific crimes that broke public and sacred laws, but their significant overarching concepts are that the state has the right to adjudicate breaches of the law and that it was the Comitia Centuriata or a consul—rather than the injured private citizen—that determined penalties.

A New Balance of Power

Perhaps the most revolutionary idea in the Twelve Tablets as a whole was that the laws applied equally to patricians and plebeians; the only exception was a provision in Tablet Eleven that prohibited marriage between plebeians and patricians. A few years later, however, even this law was overturned by the *Lex Canuleia*.

The legislative distinction between the two classes was further broken down when, around 445 B.C., the Comitia Centuriata and its patrician leaders, under pressure from an Aequian invasion and the plebeians' threatened refusal to serve in the army, agreed to grant consular powers to tribunes without their actually being consuls. Theoretically, a consul was still distinct from a consular tribune, but in effect the political power was the same. The only difference between a consular tribune and a consul was that the former was not entitled to a triumphal parade on the conclusion of a successful military campaign, nor was he automatically granted a seat in the Senate upon completion of his term of office. In 376 B.C., the Licinio-Sextian Law abolished this awkward distinction between consuls and consular tribunes and gave plebeians the right to be elected to the office of consul.

By the mid-fourth century B.C., the plebeians' quest for a degree of political equality was realized; the Roman system was now a balanced dual government

made up of plebeian and patrician branches, each able to pass laws and check the excesses of the other. On the patrician side, the consul (although in time plebeians would hold this office) could propose a law and, if his fellow consul approved, present it to the Senate. The Senate, made up mostly of patricians, gave their approval to the Comitia Centuriata, which the wealthy patricians dominated through a preferential voting procedure that favored the rich.

The plebeians, however, could enact laws as well. Any of the plebeian tribunes could make a proposal, which any other tribune could veto. If, however, the other tribunes approved, they submitted the proposed action to the Concilium Plebis Tributa, made up of all free plebeian males sixteen and older, who passed or rejected it. If the law was passed, it went to the Senate for approval and then to the Comitia Centuriata,

where a positive vote made it law. In principle, the Comitia Centuriata could reject a law sent to it by the Concilium Plebis Tributa, but to do so meant risking the displeasure of the plebeians and the military consequences that entailed.

Perhaps to counteract the growing power of the Concilium Plebis Tributa, in 366 B.C., the patricians created a new legislative body called the *Comitia Tributa*, in which both patricians and plebeians voted as equals. The patricians probably hoped to guide the plebeians from within toward approving legislation that was friendly to patrician interests. In 339 B.C., the Comitia Tributa was permitted to pass legislation binding on the whole state if the Senate approved it. This legislation completely bypassed the Comitia Centuriata, yet instead of making the plebeians more malleable, it encouraged them further to become their own political

Rome's Neighbors and the Development of
Republican Government

masters. Some of this plebeian progress resulted from the fact that the same plebeians who served in the Comitia Tributa also served in the Concilium Plebis Tributa, and these men saw no reason to let patricians dictate to them in one assembly what they could do independently in the other. Nor did they see any reason to stop agitating for recognition of the actions of the Concilium Plebis Tributa, the exclusively plebeian assembly.

In 287 B.C., the plebeians finally had their way when the patricians gave up the struggle and allowed the Lex Hortensia to pass through the Comitia Centuriata. This law recognized the actions of both the Concilium Plebis Tributa and the Comitia Tributa without Senate approval. From then on, the Concilium Plebis Tributa was fully equal to the Comitia Centuriata; the Comitia Tributa would survive as a political body with the same status as the Comitia Curiata. The Comitia Tributa was no more than a relic of the past, limited to formally approving legislation already passed by the Concilium Plebis Tributa.

The passage of the Lex Hortensia created two totally separate governments within Rome, each of which could not only pass laws independent of the other but also check the other by passing contradictory laws. Given this strange arrangement, it might have made sense to abolish one or the other, or somehow combine them, but the conservative Romans never liked to do away with any political institution, and in fact the two branches tended to cooperate.

Rome's Neighbors and the Development of
Republican Government

OFFICES AND OFFICERS OF THE ROMAN REPUBLIC

Other changes in the Roman government developed during this period of struggle between the patricians and plebeians, although not necessarily because of that struggle. Most of the changes were intended to facilitate the work of either the popular assemblies or the officials that directed them. The most prestigious of these officials were the censors, first elected by the Comitia Centuriata in 443 B.C. to tabulate the official census and assess the taxes and military obligation of each male citizen. This relieved the two consuls of a burdensome responsibility, but also made the censors powerful officials. Around 312 B.C., the censors gained even more power with the right to approve the suitability of new senators and remove any senator from office whom they considered immoral. Censors could also deprive a citizen of his civil rights for up to five years. In the early years of the Republic, the censors served five-year terms, making their office even more influential than that of consul.

Almost equal in status with the office of censor was that of praetor. The term was originally used instead of "consul," and some early documents use the term praetor/consul; by 367 B.C., however, "praetor" designated the supreme administrator of justice in Rome. Originally there was only one praetor, but as the Roman Republic expanded throughout Italy and into the Mediterranean Basin, the number was increased to eight. Each praetor was appointed to deal with a specific area of the law, such as extortion, bribery, embezzlement, forgery, trust agreements, disputes between citizens and the treasury, the rights of minors, or the manumission of slaves. At a much later date, during the second century A.D., a praetor called the praetor urbanus would be charged with providing games to entertain the populace.

Another high official in the early Republic was the quaestor, who oversaw the treasury. Until 421 B.C., the consuls appointed two quaestors; after that, the number was increased to four, and they were elected by the Concilium Plebis Tributa. Strangely, and without any explanation, this assembly elected patricians to the office until 409 B.C., when the first plebeians were elected. Besides fiscal matters, quaestors investigated murders and robberies within Rome. Their office was in the Temple of Saturn because the state treasury and the national archives were in the basement of that building. The quaestorship was the first civil service office that a young, ambitious Roman could attain on a political path that he hoped would lead to the consulship and eventually to the Senate. (All ex-consuls were eligible to be members of that body as vacancies occurred.)

The aediles were originally two young men elected by the Concilium Plebis Tributa to assist the tribunes and to supervise the Temple of Ceres on the Aventine, where the plebeian treasury and archives were stored. In 367 B.C., the patricians decided to elect two aediles from within their own ranks, using the Comitia Tributa. The duties of these curile aediles included supervising Rome's streets, markets, and water supply and prosecuting cases of rape, fraud, usury, and insults to the plebeians. In the late Republic, two aediles were in charge of supervising the grain supply for Rome.

By the late fourth century B.C., the Roman Republic was moving toward an administrative system that appears cumbersome but provided leadership for the emerging nation. The effectiveness of the Roman government was soon to be tested against the Samnites, a formidable group of mountain dwellers living along the eastern coast of Italy.

CHAPTER III

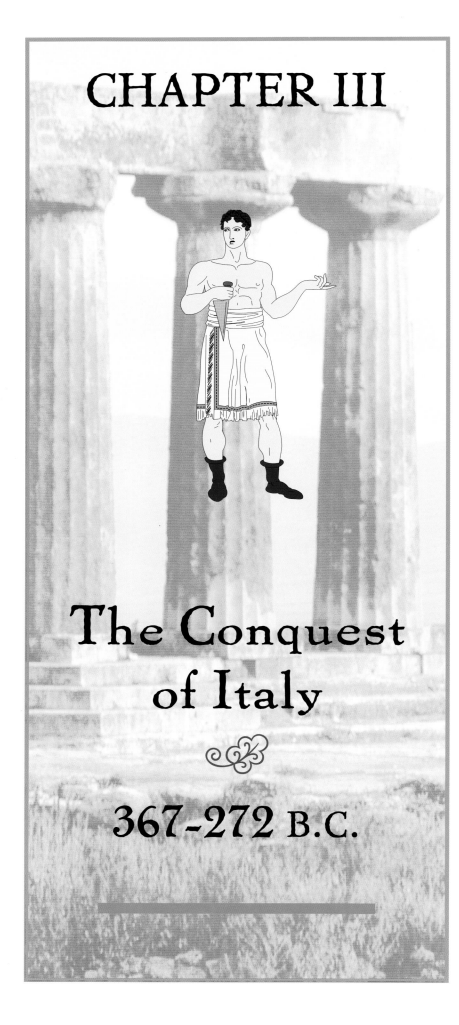

The Conquest of Italy

367-272 B.C.

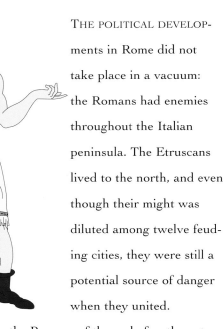

THE POLITICAL DEVELOPMENTS in Rome did not take place in a vacuum: the Romans had enemies throughout the Italian peninsula. The Etruscans lived to the north, and even though their might was diluted among twelve feuding cities, they were still a potential source of danger when they united.

Happily for the Romans of the early fourth century B.C., the Etruscan threat was further disrupted by the Gallic incursions. Although the Gauls had retreated from Rome in 380 B.C., they had certainly not withdrawn from Italy but instead settled in the plains of the Po River, whence they continued to raid south into Etruscan territory and occasionally as far south as Latium. In 360, 359, and 349 B.C., the Gauls sent raiding parties into Latium, their fierceness spreading absolute panic among the Romans. Soon after the last of these three raids, the Romans instituted a special tax upon themselves called the *aerarium sanctius*, earmarked exclusively for fighting the Gauls. In terror and desperation, the Romans also reverted to ancient practices: in 288 B.C. they offered the gods human sacrifices, burying a Gallic and a Greek couple alive in the *Forum Boarium*.

The greatest threat to Rome in the mid-fourth century B.C.—even more than from the Etruscans and Gauls—came from the Samnites. These were an Oscan-speaking people who lived on the slopes of the Apennines to the east of Latium and whose culture spread to the Adriatic coast and from the Po plains south to Apulia. The Samnites inhabited small villages grouped into loose political units called *pagi*. In time of war or external danger, the Samnites united into a federation, placing themselves voluntarily under the leadership of a supreme commander.

Throughout most of Rome's growth to dominance in Latium, the Samnites had been content with occasional forays into Roman territory, looking for loot. In 354 B.C., they signed a treaty with the Romans, and relations remained peaceable until 343, when conditions deteriorated to the point that the two nations were at war off and on for nearly fifty years.

THE FIRST SAMNITE WAR

The First Samnite War began in 343 B.C., allegedly because the Samnites attacked the Campanian town of Capua. Historians have never explained why Rome should have been concerned with a Samnite attack on a Greek city so far from Rome, but one possible explanation is that the Romans regarded the Samnite attack as a threat to their trade with the Greek cities of Neapolis (modern Naples) and Cumae on the Tyrrhenian coast. A Roman army marched to Capua, relieved the siege, and stayed on as a garrison force. Trouble quickly developed when the Roman troops became unruly, threatening to rebel and even turn around and march on Rome. The cause of discontent was apparently boredom and homesickness: the Romans soldiers had never been so far from home for so long.

Livy, the only source of historical information about this war, blames the trouble on the wickedly immoral climate of Campania. To the puritanical Romans, the Campanian cities were notorious haunts of sexual license and strange foreign ideas that could corrupt the simple but honest Roman soldiers of the occupation forces. In any event, the discontent of the army became so great that the Romans made peace with the Samnites. The Samnites, in turn, were only too glad to end the fighting because they were nervous over the arrival of a Spartan mercenary captain named Archidamnus at the Greek town of Tarentum (modern Taranto). Tarentum, an urban commercial center situated on the coast of the instep of Italy's "boot," was a traditional enemy of the Samnites, who often raided the territory of their more settled neighbors. The appearance of a trained body of mercenary soldiers in Tarentum frightened the Samnites, who foresaw the possibility of fighting a war on two fronts—against the Romans to the north and the Greeks to the south.

Once the Romans were free of the Samnite menace, the Roman consul Marcus Valerius Corvus personally appealed to the mutinous Roman soldiers and quickly brought the disorder to an end. Unfortunately, this evidence of dissension among the Romans led to further complications. Some of the Latin cities allied to Rome were disaffected, believing that Rome was beginning to treat them as subjects rather than as equals; they may also have perceived the rapid expansion of Rome throughout Latium as a potential threat. They now saw an opportunity to break away—and took it.

It took the Roman armies nearly four years to defeat these allied cities, but when the war ended in 337 B.C. with a Roman victory, the Romans resisted the temptation to punish the rebels severely. Instead, realizing that repression breeds resentment, they defused the feelings of resentment, first by granting wholesale pardons and then by offering favorable terms to the defeated cities. The terms differed, however, according to the individual cases of the cities: while all the citizens of some cities received grants of Roman citizenship, some cities became self-governing *municipii*,

surrendering their independence only with respect to foreign relations with other cities. Most of the defeated cities received the *commercium*, or right to trade freely with Rome, and the *conubium*, the right to marry freely into Roman families. All cities had to supply troops on demand to the Roman army in times of war, but along with this obligation came the right to a share of any plunder that the forces under Roman command gathered, including a portion of any territory conquered from an enemy in a joint military venture with Rome.

Rome established colonies on conquered land throughout central Italy. These colonies, garrisoned with settlers from Rome's allied cities, gave these cities a tremendous opportunity to settle their surplus population on rich farmland and gave to Rome settlers at strategic points who had every reason to remain loyal to such a generous benefactor. The wisdom of these humane and intelligent policies toward the Roman allies was validated in succeeding years when foreign

The Conquest of Italy

49

invaders found it nearly impossible to induce allied Italian cities to renege on their allegiance to Rome.

THE SECOND SAMNITE WAR

While Rome's colonial policy might have gained her friends among some Italian peoples, the same policy unfortunately caused further difficulties with the Samnites. In 328 B.C., some twelve years after the end of the First Samnite War, Rome found herself once again at war with the Samnites, this time over a newly established Roman colony at Fregellae, on the Liris River about seventy miles (112.5km) southeast of Rome. Ever since they had conquered the Liris River Valley from the Volscans ten years before, the Samnites fiercely regarded this territory as their own. A demand for Roman withdrawal brought only a Roman counteroffer of negotiation, which the Samnites contemptuously refused by challenging the Romans to meet them on "the fields of Campania. . .where [they both] could decide who would rule Italy." The Samnites went from words to action; they supposedly

persuaded the Greeks of Neapolis to attack some Roman colonies in Campania, so Rome found herself involved in a twenty-year war with the Samnites.

The Romans fought the Samnites in the Second Samnite War in two distinct intervals. From 328 to 321 B.C., the Romans invaded Samnium, initially winning several battles. In 321, however, a Roman army, trapped in a narrow pass called the Caudine Forks, was obliged to submit to a shameful peace: the Samnites forced the Romans to throw down their weapons and armor, strip down to their shirts, and walk under a yoke made of two spears stuck in the ground with a third tied across as a lintel. Even though the Romans had surrendered, the Samnites slaughtered a few of their defeated enemies as they passed under this arch because their faces did not show "adequate humility." Rome reluctantly agreed to a five-year peace on humiliating terms, including the loss of their colonies at Fregellae and nearby Sora.

Rome did not waste these five years. For the first time in their long history, the Romans demonstrated one of their most characteristic behaviors in defeat. Refusing to accept the status quo, they immediately turned to organizing their resources with an eye toward reentering the conflict in the future with an unbeatable military and diplomatic strength. Rome, throughout her long history, was stubbornly tenacious—once the Romans determined a course they pursued it, no matter what the cost, to complete victory.

On the diplomatic front, the Romans began to create alliances with the Lucanians and Apulians, people living to the south of the Samnites; at the same time, the Romans increased their hold on their allies in Campania while reinforcing the cities of southern Latium on the Samnite frontier. The Romans' goal— to surround the Samnites—was simple but effective.

The Conquest of Italy

The New Roman Legions

Around 311 B.C., the Romans carried out important changes in the organization of their armies. They not only increased the size of their army from two to four legions but also began a complete tactical reorganization of these military forces. Until then, the Roman armies, like most other Mediterranean military powers of the era, had organized their soldiers into tight phalanxes that concentrated the power into a strong push at the front of the line. This system, however, worked well only on level, open ground near the coast; it was totally unsuited for combat in irregular terrain or on mountains, such as those at the heartland of Samnium. It is evidence of their military genius that the Romans were able to develop a tactical formation that could function effectively on both types of terrain.

This new organization, named for the *manipulus*, its basic unit, not only allowed greater flexibility on the battlefield but also provided a more solid defensive arrangement that could withstand both the formal phalanxes of Rome's coastal enemies and the wild, disorganized charges that characterized mountain warfare. A Roman legion was now divided into thirty manipuli. A manipulus could operate either independantly or in conjunction with other manipuli. This flexibilty allowed for rapid battlefield changes to meet different kinds of enemy formations.

Roman armor consisted of visorless bronze helmets fitting closely over the ears and completely covering the back of the head. The soldiers also wore a bronze breastplate and greaves, which extended from slightly above the knee down to the ankle. The most important piece of armor, however, was the rectangular shield that protected a soldier from the top of his helmet to his knees. These shields were made of two layers of wood glued together, covered with leather, and edged with an iron band. When well-trained Roman soldiers advanced to attack or stood on the defensive, each man interlocked the edge of his shield with that of the men on either side to present an unbroken wall.

The sides of a manipulus were also protected: soldiers carried their shields on their left or right when marching and at right angles to the soldiers facing front during an attack. Should the situation deteriorate to the point where a manipulus was totally isolated from a legion and surrounded on all sides, the rear rank could turn completely around, presenting an unbroken wall at the rear of the formation. Soldiers within a manipulus could raise their shields over their heads to present a protective roof against an enemy's arrows or rocks. When shields protected a manipulus at the front, at the rear, on the sides, and on the top, it was called a *testudo*, or turtle, and functioned as a kind of ancient tank that could slowly and in relative safety advance or retreat across a battlefield.

With the manipulus formation, the Romans had developed a military tactical formation that served them on the open plains of Campania as well as on the mountainous slopes of Samnium. A legion could be defeated, but usually only when the troops were not trained well enough to hold their formations, or else when a Roman army was surprised in the field before it could form into ranks.

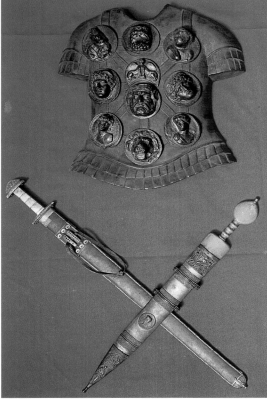

Although the armor and swords are from a much later period than the Samnite Wars, they demonstrate the Roman dedication to constantly changing and improving their military capabilities. The metal chest armor, or cuirasse, was at first made of bronze, but by the second century A.D. steel was used. Roman swords were short instruments designed to facilitate stabbing—rather than slashing—for use by troops partially concealed behind the large standardized shields of the Roman army.

When the war resumed in 316 B.C., the Romans were in an excellent position to threaten the Samnites within their own territory. Simultaneous attacks from the north, south, and west pushed deeply into Samnite territory, and by 313 B.C., the Romans had reconquered Fregellae and Sora and conquered a string of fortified cities on the Samnite-Lucanian frontier. Roman armies drove the Samnites out of Campania and reinforced their hold on this important area by undertaking construction of Rome's first military road, the Appian Way, which ran south from Rome to Capua. This was the first of the many surfaced, all-weather roads that connected the Roman world and allowed for supplies and troops to move easily and relatively quickly.

THE THIRD SAMNITE WAR AND VICTORY

The surviving sources do not give a precise account of the events of the Samnite war after 316 B.C. Livy and another historian, Dionysius of Halicarnassus, supply a swirl of battles and dates that often contradict each other and that, consequently, historians have been unable to form into a coherent whole. A general picture emerges, however, of the Romans annually invading Samnium and of the Samnites launching periodic attacks into the plains of Campania. Around 304 B.C. the Samnites, at the conclusion of a particularly successful season of Roman campaigning, asked for a peace treaty, and the Romans agreed.

This ready compliance with the Samnite request appears to have been caused by a sudden resurgence of activity on the part of the Etruscans. For nearly forty years the Romans had been able to rely on the squabbling between the principal Etruscan cities to keep these northern neighbors of Rome from threatening Latium.

But around 311 B.C., at least five Etruscan cities formed a military alliance that was also able to enlist Umbrian tribes that lived northeast of Rome. The determined enemies encircled Rome. Luckily for the Romans, though, Caere, Tarquinia, and Vulci—the most powerful of the Etruscan cities along Italy's west coast—did not join this most recent Etruscan alliance. In spite of being surrounded by enemies, the Romans apparently won more battles than they lost and even expanded their territory at the expense of both the Etruscans and the Umbrians. To consolidate their conquests in the central Apennines, the Romans built the Via Valeria that crossed the mountains to the Adriatic coast.

By 304 B.C., the Romans controlled a large territory that included not only Latium but also a large section of the central Apennines and most of Campania down to Neapolis. As the largest political entity in Italy, Rome presented a threat to the peninsula's other inhabitants, who took steps to protect their interests. In 298, the Samnites, Umbrians, Gauls, and inhabitants of many of the Etruscan cities joined forces with the sole purpose of destroying Rome. The Roman government responded by extending the term of the consuls and praetors who commanded the armies past the usual year. This was dramatic proof that the Romans felt imperiled by the quadruple alliance, since they tended to be extremely cautious about granting substantial military power to any individual for too long.

In 295 B.C. an allied army made up of Gauls and Samnites moved north to hook up with an army of Etruscans and Umbrians; the combined forces engaged the Romans at Sentinum, in north central Umbria. The Battle of Sentinum was the largest battle fought in Italy up to that time, and historians agree that the Roman army, led jointly by the consuls Publius Decius Mus and Quintus Fabius, consisted

of four legions numbering perhaps thirty-six thousand men; the Gallic-Samnite forces, commanded by Gellius Egnatius, were slightly more numerous. Livy reports that the enemy originally outnumbered the Romans two to one, but that the Etruscan and Umbrian contingents were drawn north into Etruria when two Roman legions advanced out of Rome to threaten the cities of Perusia and Clusium.

When the Romans met the Samnites and the Gauls at Sentinum, the battle swept back and forth across the field for most of the day, with the Roman manipuli more than holding their own against an enemy fighting in a close pack. However, at a critical moment the Gauls attacked the Roman cavalry with chariots, just as the Romans were attacking their left flank. The chariots drove hard into the Roman right flank, causing the Roman infantry to panic. At this point, the consul Publius Decius Mus rallied some of the cavalry and led a suicidal charge into the Gauls that checked their advance but cost him his life. His heroic example inspired the Romans but also gave them time to reform the manipuli and return to the attack. Late in the day, according to Livy, Quintus Fabius, the surviving consul, ordered his cavalry to attack both flanks of the enemy, precipitating havoc in their ranks. Whether or not it was true, Livy claims that Quintus Fabius had been waiting for an opportunity to attack late in the day because he knew from past experience that the Gauls and Samnites did not have the staying power to fight for an extended period of time. Whatever the case, faced with advancing Roman infantry from the front and Roman cavalry crashing into both flanks, the Samnite and Gallic forces broke and fled. The Roman cavalry in pursuit cut down thousands: Livy claims that the enemy lost twenty-five thousand men during and after the battle,

while the Romans lost eight thousand. As inordinately large as these figures may seem, they are consistent with other ancient battle statistics.

The Battle of Samnium broke the back of the Samnite resistance, and they surrendered in 290 B.C. The Gauls attempted an invasion of Latium in 284, but were decisively defeated in 283 at the Battle of Lake Vadimon, about sixty miles (96.5km) north of Rome. The Etruscan cities that had opposed Rome held out a little longer, but were defeated one by one between 280 and 264; they were incorporated into the Republic under favorable terms, and their inhabitants became Roman citizens. Rome was the undisputed master of central—but not southern—Italy.

ROME, MAGNA GRAECIA, AND PYRRHUS OF EPIRUS

Colonists from mainland Greece had settled in Italy 450 years earlier, especially on the southern coastline, where now Greek-speaking cities thrived on trade with the western Mediterranean and the Italian interior. So strong was the Greek influence in this area that the Romans referred to the whole area of southern Italy and Sicily as Magna Graecia, or Great Greece. Greek-speaking cities of this region such as Neapolis, Cumae, Heraclea, Paestum, Rhegium (modern Reggio Calabria), Thurii, and Tarentum looked upon the non-Greek-speaking Italian cities as cultural and economic backwaters, but were happy to trade with the Etruscans north of Rome for their iron ore.

For centuries, the Greek cities had fought to keep the mountaineers of the Italian interior at bay. Greek wealth lured these barbarians—a barbarian was anyone who didn't speak Greek—to raid the coastal plains. Usually, the highly trained phalanxes of the Greek cities had been more than adequate for defense, and these cities had no real territorial ambitions with regard to the Italian interior. Rome's rise and consolidation of central Italy caused the Greeks to notice her diplomatically. As early as 303 B.C., Tarentum, the powerful Greek colony of Sparta, negotiated a treaty with Rome. Rome agreed to stay out of the Gulf of Tarentum if the Tarentians did not trade along the west coast of Italy. Thurii, an Athenian colony directly across the Bay of Tarentum from Tarentum, even contracted a mutual defense treaty with Rome in 285.

Conditions did not remain peaceful for long between Rome and Tarentum, however. In 282 B.C. a fleet of ten Roman warships entered Tarentian waters, and the Greeks promptly sank four of them. In retaliation for this treaty violation, Tarentum launched an attack on and conquered Rome's ally Thurii. The Romans sent an envoy, Lucius Postumius Megellus, to protest, but the Tarentum assembly mocked his Greek pronunciation and he returned to Rome recommending war. The Romans sent an army south, laid siege to the city, and forced it to sue for peace. Angry over the Roman attack, the Tarentians decided to employ a mercenary army to teach the upstart Romans a lesson.

Pyrrhus of Epirus (319–272 B.C.), chosen to lead the Greeks, was the greatest threat the Romans had faced since the Gallic attack on Rome more than a century before. Pyrrhus, king of Epirus, had received his military training campaigning with Alexander the Great; for the first time, the Romans would face professional soldiers using phalanx tactics. Pyrrhus arrived in Tarentum in 280 B.C. with a formidable army of twenty-five thousand infantry, three thousand cavalry—and twenty elephants. The Greeks had first encountered war elephants at the Battle of Gaugamela in 331, when the Persian king Darius' army included troops from India. After that date, elephants—animate tanks—became a regular part of the Ptolemaic armies; Pyrrhus undoubtedly learned their military value during his stay in Egypt. Each elephant bore a howdah, a small armored structure that carried two soldiers armed with javelins; a mahout controlled the elephant. The principal military impact of the elephants, however, was not the soldiers in the howdah but the very size of the animal, whose thick hide served as a kind of armor against enemy spears, as the great beast plowed through an opposing line. Elephants were especially useful against cavalry, since horses have an instinctive fear of elephants unless they are specially trained to overcome this fear.

The First Defeat

The Romans discovered horses' natural fear of elephants at the Battle of Heraclea. When Pyrrhus sent his elephants against the Roman horsemen, the animals panicked, turned around, and drove into the Roman

Left: The famous bust of King Pyrrhus of Epirus (319–272 B.C.) is probably a realistic representation of the king's features, even to the deformity of his mouth. Although a brillant tactician, Pyrrhus lacked the stamina for protracted campaigns, a fact that helped save the early Roman Republic from a disastrous defeat. Pyrrhus died during an attack on Argos when he was struck in the head by a roof tile thrown by an old woman.

The Conquest of Italy

Above: This terra-cotta sculpture of a Punic War elephant depicts the fighting tower, or *howdah*, as a stone one, but it would actually have been composed of wood and leather, and its driver, or *mahout*, would have controlled the elephant from the inside. The tower would also have held several archers.

infantry. The carefully trained manipuli gave way, allowing Pyrrhus' own cavalry to wreak further disorder and disintegration in the Roman ranks. The whole Roman army might have been destroyed had it not been for the manipular formations. In an emergency such as this, a manipulus, with its walls of interlocking shields, became a self-contained military unit that could maneuver independently of the rest of the army. Cavalry units could slaughter fleeing troops, but they had to proceed with caution against a solid wall of Roman shields.

Nevertheless, the number of Roman deaths must have been considerable, although the ancient authors differ about exactly how many Romans died. Whatever the exact figures, the Roman losses were substantial enough to urge many Roman senators to consider Pyrrhus' peace offer. Only the firm resistance of the venerable Appius Claudius Caecus prevented a senatorial stampede toward peace, and Pyrrhus' ambassador was sent home.

An Honorable Adversary

Plutarch, the famous first-century A.D. biographer of many notable Greeks and Romans, tells us that the Romans were genuinely fond of Pyrrhus, and he in turn was certainly respectful toward the Romans. He praised their courage and discipline, at the same time publicly criticizing the soft ways and undisciplined behavior of his Tarentian allies. When the Romans sent the consul Gaius Fabricius to negotiate the ransom of Roman soldiers captured at Heraclea, he and Pyrrhus struck up a friendship. Pyrrhus even sent the Roman prisoners back to Rome with the proviso that if the Senate did not vote for peace, the captive soldiers would be returned to him. When the Senate rejected Pyrrhus' second peace offer, Fabricius honorably sent the prisoners back to captivity.

The good relations between Fabricius and Pyrrhus continued throughout the war. At one point, Fabricius received a letter from Pyrrhus' physician offering to poison the king for a considerable bribe. Fabricius not only refused but sent the letter to Pyrrhus, who promptly executed the traitorous doctor. In thanks, Pyrrhus allowed all his Roman prisoners to return to Rome without ransom—an act that prompted the Romans to return all the Greek POWs free of charge.

A Costly Victory

Despite some limited diplomatic successes, the war continued. In 279 B.C., when the Romans sent yet another army against Pyrrhus, the two forces met at Asculum, about 250 miles (402km) northwest of Tarentum. Although in the early stages of the battle the Roman manipuli drove back the Greek phalanx, the elephants once again carried the day. They thundered into the Roman ranks, and as Plutarch tells it, the Romans felt as if they were in the midst of an earthquake, and their formations fell back. Instead of being routed, they retreated to their fortified camp. Hieronymus claims that six thousand Romans

The Conquest of Italy

and thirty-five hundred Greeks died. Pyrrhus was wounded, and a party of Samnites, apparently operating as bandits and not part of the Roman army, pillaged the Greek supply train. At the end of this battle, Pyrrhus uttered his famous remark that "another such victory would mean defeat," giving origin to the phrase a "Pyrrhic victory," meaning a victory so costly that it means defeat for the winner.

So discouraged was Pyrrhus with his war against the Romans that when, in 278 B.C., ambassadors from the Sicilian cities of Agrigentum (modern Agrigento), Syracusae (modern Syracuse), and Leontini (modern Lentini) arrived begging Pyrrhus to enlist his army in their fight against the Carthaginians, he gladly accepted the offer and moved his army to Sicily. The Tarentians were now on their own against the Romans, who launched a punitive campaign against Tarentum. Within three years, the Romans had laid siege to Tarentum, and the Tarentians begged Pyrrhus to come back.

Their frantic appeal reached Pyrrhus just when he was becoming sick of the war in Sicily. His disgust was due less to the military skill of the Carthaginians than to the duplicity of the Sicilians, who refused to support him as they had promised. In 275, therefore, he accepted the invitation of Tarentum once more, and returned to Italy for one more chance to defeat Rome.

This time the two armies met at Malventum ("bad wind") on the Volturnus River, about 130 miles (209km) southeast of Rome. Hoping to take them unprepared at dawn, Pyrrhus tried an unconventional night march against the Roman camp. His army became lost and arrived at the Roman camp well after dawn, thus losing the element of surprise. The ensuing battle would be different, for the Romans had used the three years since Asculum to train both their cavalry

Below: A mural depicts the blind Appius Claudius Caecus being led into the Senate. There he would make a speech against the proposed peace treaty with Pyrrhus after the terrible Roman defeat at Heraclea in 280 B.C.

Below: A mural depicts the blind Appius Claudius Caecus being led into the Senate. There he would make a speech against the proposed peace treaty with Pyrrhus after the terrible Roman defeat at Heraclea in 280 B.C.

The Conquest of Italy

horses and their infantry to fight against elephants. When Pyrrhus attacked, the Romans withdrew into trenches, which allowed them—although Plutarch does not tell us exactly how—to drive back the advancing elephants. The huge beasts were driven back into the Greek army, which had been advancing a second rank of elephants behind the first. At that point, the Roman cavalry and infantry attacked the disorganized Greeks, and for once Pyrrhus was on the losing side. The Romans commemorated their victory at Malventum by changing the name of the town to Beneventum, or "good wind."

Pyrrhus retreated to Tarentum, where he left a small Greek garrison, and embarked his army for Epirus, never to return. Meanwhile, back in Italy, the Romans continued their campaign against Tarentum, finally conquering the city in 272 B.C. They spent the next nine years reducing those Samnites and Lucanians who had supported Pyrrhus, and by 263, the Romans controlled all of Italy from the Arnus (modern Arno) River to the tips of the peninsula's "toe" and "heel."

The Roman defeat of Pyrrhus caught the attention of the Mediterranean world, which had considered Pyrrhus the military equal of Alexander the Great. Ptolemy II (r. 285–246 B.C.)—whose father, Ptolemy I (r. 323–285 B.C.), had been one of Alexander's chief generals—sent an embassy to Rome in 272 to make a treaty of friendship with this emerging young politi-cal power. The Romans, in return, sent a senatorial delegation to Egypt. In Athens, the historian Timaeus of Tauromenium (c. 350–260 B.C.) wrote a popular account, which unfortunately has not survived, of the war between Pyrrhus and the Romans. This account allowed the Greeks to became familiar with their new neighbors.

NEW MONEY

The conquest of so large an area in a series of wars that lasted for 108 years had profound consquences for Rome. Not only did it make Rome a major military power in the Mediterranean, but it would forever alter Roman society by creating an unaccustomed amount of wealth for the Romans and their Republic. It was during the wars against the Samnites that individual Romans began to acquire large country estates and farms in the recently conquered territories. T.J. Cornell, the chief authority on the development of Rome from the sixth through third centuries B.C., estimates in his book *Beginnings of Rome* that in 338 B.C., at the end of the wars with the Latins, Roman territory covered some 2,100 square miles (5,439 sq km). By 264, after the defeat of the Samnites, Etruscans, Umbrians, Pyrrhus and his Greeks, and others, the Roman Republic and its conquests extended to about 10,350 square miles (26,807 sq km).

The Romans shared some of this new land with their loyal allies and divided the rest among their own people, including the lower classes of Roman citizens, who spread out over the newly conquered territory to farm small plots. It is no coincidence that toward the end of the third century B.C. there are fewer and fewer references to plebeians being enslaved for debt.

A CHANGE OF WAYS

Although the abundance from this new land made certain Romans rich, the Romans of a later date preserved the legend that during this period of strife, their austere forefathers enjoyed the simple rustic life and disdained luxury. For instance, in the first century A.D., when Plutarch wrote admiringly about these early Romans, he repeated a story about the Samnite ambassadors who came to negotiate with the consul Manius Curius Denatus. The ambassadors found Manius Curius cooking a simple meal of turnips at home, a simple peasant hut. When they offered him gold with which to buy a better house and food, he refused, explaining that it was more honorable to live simply than to take gold from the enemies of Rome.

The houses of the period are no different from those of the early Republic, except they are larger; archaeology has also uncovered expensive artworks made for individuals and indicating surplus wealth. The tombs, too, evince individual wealth: the earliest examples of Roman fresco work come from the tomb of Quintus Fabius Rullianus, a hero of the Second Samnite War. The sarcophagus of Lucius Cornelius Scipio Barbarus, one of the consuls in 298 B.C., is imposingly ornate and was obviously expensive.

Perhaps most impressive of all is the magnificent bronze bust of an unknown Roman nobleman, known to archaeologists as the Capitoline Brutus because it was found on the Capitoline—although there is no hard evidence at all that the sitter was named Brutus. A short beard and close-cropped hair surround a narrow face with piercing eyes that suggest a stern, unbending will, calling to mind Plutarch's famous quote about Lucius Junius Brutus, "a man of steel with a character unsoftened by thought or study."

It is, almost certainly, a portrait because no ancient artist ever sculpted a deity or hero with the wrinkles, sharp nose, and puffy eyes that this head displays. The Capitoline Brutus is surely an archetype of the magnificent portrait busts that became popular in the first century B.C. and remained hallmarks of Roman art to the end of the Empire.

Other surviving pieces are evidence of Rome's flourishing bronze industry at this time. A bronze cista, or toiletry container, from Praeneste, some twenty miles (32km) east of Rome, bears two inscriptions: "Given by Dindia Macolnia to her daughter" and (on the handle) "Made in Rome by Novios Plautios." This work is surely representative of a craftsman who produced luxury items for rich Roman citizens.

THE GRANDEUR THAT WAS ROME

While some Romans increased their fortunes, the state benefited from the conquest of foreign lands through the plunder and tribute it collected from its defeated enemies. No accounting of the amount of loot that the Romans brought home survives, but some concept of its extent may be inferred from the number of temples publicly funded during this period of Roman expansion. For instance, the historian T.J. Cornell writes that fourteen major temples were built in Rome between 302 and 264 B.C., to which the contemporary Roman literature also attests. This boom in temple construction and in the number of aqueducts, roads, fortifications, and government buildings makes the decades at the end of the fourth century and the beginning of the third century second only to the building campaigns of the emperor Augustus between 27 B.C. and A.D. 14.

The Conquest of Italy

Temples of War and Healing

In 296 B.C. a new temple was raised in honor of Bellona Victrix, a goddess of war and the sister of Mars. At a critical moment in a battle against the Samnites and Etruscans, the consul Appius Claudius Caecus called upon the goddess Bellona to increase the courage of his troops in their assault on the enemy's fortified camp. When the Romans burst over the defensive trenches and ramparts and killed or captured nearly ten thousand of the enemy, Appius felt he owed a debt of gratitude to Bellona. He financed the foundation of the temple with the spoils of that skirmish.

This temple stood in the Campus Martius, where the Roman legions trained and where the Senate met foreign ambassadors or victorious Roman generals following a successful campaign. The Romans built the temple outside the sacred pomerium, a strip of land just outside the walls of Rome where no military actions were permitted to take place. The Senate had to meet beyond the pomerium whenever they discussed hostilities.

The fetiales, or war priests, also met at this temple to discuss questions of war and peace. In the early days of the city, when Rome's enemies were close at hand, a fetialis actually traveled to the boundary of the Roman state and shouted the reason for Rome's grievance across the border. In later days the rapidly expanding circle of Rome's enemies made this impossible, and the fetialis made the martial announcement into the space immediately in front of the *Columna Bellica*, which was, symbolically, enemy territory. If the proposed enemy did not offer a convincing reason against war within thirty-three days, the fetialis returned to the Columna Bellica and cast a spear into "enemy territory," whereupon Rome was at war.

Wars also ended in the Temple of Bellona Victrix. When the fetiales accepted a peace treaty, they followed a reading of the proposed treaty in the temple with a curse upon the Roman state if the Romans were to break the treaty. The fetiales then sacrificed a pig with a sacred stone knife, the lapis silex, and the war was officially over.

The Temple of Aesculapius was erected on tiny Tiber Island after a plague raged through the city between 293 and 292 B.C. After the epidemic had run its course, the Senate, hoping to ensure that such a terrible thing would never happen again, resolved to build a temple to the god of the healing arts. They

HOUSES OF THE GODS

Few of the many temples paid for with spoils of war have survived, but the accounts of Livy and other historians tell us of them. The Romans were pious people whose temples acknowledged the importance of the gods in their private lives and in the affairs of the Republic. The first known temple to Venus was constructed during this period. The Romans considered Venus their special protector and frequently implored her to intervene with her foster father, Jupiter, on behalf of the Republic. A temple was built to Tellus, the goddess of cultivated fields, on the Esquiline. The Temple of Salus, the goddess of the safety and welfare of the state, sat on the Quirinal. The hill itself was originally named dispatched Gallus Quintus Ogulnius and a delegation of senators to bring back holy paraphernalia from the Temple of Asclepius—the Greek form of the god's name—in Epidaurus in southeast Greece. As the Roman delegation was standing in the temple before the statue of Asclepius, a huge snake emerged from behind the figure and slithered across the floor and out of the temple. Since snakes were traditionally associated with Asclepius, the visitors interpreted this as an omen, gathered up the creature, and carried it back to Rome. (One of the god's attributes is a staff, which with two snakes winding around it forms the caduceus, familiar to us today as the symbol of the medical profession.) As the ship approached the wharf at Rome, the snake slid off the ship into the water, swam to Tiber Island, and crawled up onto it— a sign that the temple was to be built there.

The Romans raised the temple at the southern end of the island, following the tradition of the asclepeia of the Greek world. At the center of the temple, hidden from public view by high walls, were the sleep sanctuaries, where the afflicted spent a night in a

The Temple of Aesculapius once stood on this small island in the Tiber that the Romans referred to simply as the Insula. Today, a hospital (visible in the photograph) still heals the sick on the same island.

ritual sleep ceremony. In the best case, the ritual resulted in a dream in which the god Aesculapius either revealed to the patient how to cure the disease or performed a magical cure in the course of the vision. Patients also believed that they could be cured by allowing themselves to be licked by the temple's sacred snakes. In the morning, the patient was expected to leave an offering to the god.

for an early Roman god, Quirinus, later identified with Romulus, the founder of the city. (Today, the Quirinal Palace is the Italian equivalent of the White House.)

The Aventine boasted the Temple of Consus, the god of the grainery; this was where the farmers brought the first fruits of the harvest. Roman law dictated that horses and donkeys were entitled to rest on

Consus' feast days, August 21 and December 15. A temple was erected in the Circus Maximus to Summanus, the god of midnight; wheel-shaped sweet cakes were offered and black animals sacrificed on August 13, Summanus' feast day. A temple to Vertumnus, the god of booksellers and shopkeepers, stood on the Aventine. Other deities honored with

The Conquest of Italy

Right: One of the most famous and best preserved Roman aqueducts in Europe, this one spans the Gard River near the southern French town of Nimes. It carries water 31 miles (50km) yet only drops 56 feet (17m) in that whole distance. **Opposite:** Once Rome began issuing coins about 310 B.C., the government used them for propaganda. These examples extol the contributions of four Roman politicians, including the first emperor Augustus, at the top.

temples during this time were Minerva, Fortuna (chance), Saturn, Juno, Sancus (good faith), Portunus (seaports), Hercules, and Concordia (harmony).

MIRACLES OF ENGINEERING

Other monuments besides the temples advertised Rome's new wealth and power to itself and to visiting ambassadors. Chief among these were two aqueducts built in 312 and 272 B.C. to supply water to Rome. The Romans did not invent these conduits—ruins remain from eighth-century Assyria and sixth-century Greece—but the Roman aqueducts were unique in using pipes supported high above the ground by beautifully proportioned arches. Many examples have survived the centuries: one of the best examples is Provence's famous Pont du Gard, while the aqueduct at Segovia, Spain, is still in use. Most of the course of an aqueduct, however, is underground, requiring intensive boring through mountains; furthermore, the

distribution of water was more than a simple matter of letting water flow downhill. At various points, complicated inverted siphon fixtures, or U-tubes, used the force of the stream of water descending on one side to raise the level of the water on the other.

The water was carried either in clay pipes that were made in a standardized mold and sealed at the joints with putty or in a channel made from close-fitting bricks lined with mortar. Once the water reached the city, it went through a system of settling tanks to remove the mud and small rocks, and from there to a water tower that distributed the water through smaller pipes to fountains throughout the city. Only a few Romans were actually rich enough at any time during the Republic to have water piped into their homes. These rich Romans received water through special hookups to the water towers—pipes that were set high up in the tower—so that if the water level fell, their supply would be the first to decrease or be shut off while the public fountains continued to receive their supply.

The Conquest of Italy

The first of the famous Roman roads was built during this time, and the roads would prove to be one of the factors that contributed to trade and travel but most importantly to further military successes, allowing as they did for the rapid dispatch of Roman troops into enemy territory. The popular image of Roman roads includes magnificent stone spans bridging them, but this was not always the case. The Via Appia, for example, crossed the Liris River (modern Garigliano) by a wooden bridge that was in continuous use for about eight hundred years. The volume of water at that point never decreases, so the Roman engineers could never construct the impressive stone footings needed to support an arched roadway.

COINAGE

The Romans' new wealth also gave rise to the city's first formal coinage. Although various Mediterranean civilizations had minted coins from about 700 B.C. on, Rome struck no coins of her own until the time of the wars in Campania. Apparently, the Romans either bartered or used metal weights and foreign coins until they needed an equitable means of dividing loot among the soldiers. Rather than attempting to distribute captured silver and bronze vessels of different sizes and weights, they seem to have decided to melt the metal down and mint coins of the same size.

The first Roman coins were issued not even in Rome but in Campania, soon after the Romans subjugated that area, around 310 B.C. They were composed of bronze and of silver; the bronze coins had the head of Apollo on one side and a figure resembling a minotaur on the other, along with the word "Rome" stamped in Greek letters. Silver coins from this period display, on one side, a man wearing a helmet and, on the other,

the word "ROMANO" below a horse's head. Neither coin has ever been found in archaeological sites in Rome—only in sites near Naples and Capua.

Around 270 B.C., however, toward the end of the Pyrrhic wars, the Romans issued a silver coin showing Apollo on one side and a galloping horse on the other. (They also issued bronze coins in four fractional sizes.) This was the famous as, which would remain the standard Roman coin. These asses came in four denominated sizes, the smallest of which, the quadrans, or quarter of an as, weighed 2.8 ounces (81g) and was the lowest-value coin the Romans would ever issue. A vulgar expression for a woman of low virtue was a *quadrantaria*, or "quarter of an as woman"—the exact equivalent of "two-bit whore."

A FORCE TO BE RECKONED WITH

By the end of the third century B.C., Rome had evolved from a settlement of rustic huts gathered around a river crossing to the preeminent power in Italy south of the Po. Her people enjoyed the fruits of conquest, the treasury was full, and the earlier social stresses that had divided the Republic into two hostile classes had been largely alleviated—first by the political compromises between patricians and plebeians, and second because of the wealth brought in by military conquests. Rome's record of conquests and military prowess caused foreign nations to acknowledge her power. In 306 B.C., Rhodes sent ambassadors to Rome to ask for aid in suppressing piracy. In 348 and again in 305, Carthage felt it expedient to enter into a treaty with Rome that defined their respective spheres of influence. Carthage, long the dominant commercial and military power in the western Mediterranean, was becoming nervous about the city on the Tiber.

The Conquest of Italy

CHAPTER IV

The War with Carthage and the Struggle for the Western Mediterranean

272-202 B.C.

WHILE ROME STRUGGLED for dominance in central Italy, three other powers watched attentively from the sidelines: Carthage, the former Phoenician colony in North Africa that now occupied western Sicily; Syracuse, a Greek city that dominated eastern Sicily; and the kingdom of Macedonia, which lay across the Adriatic Sea from Italy. Of the three, Carthage—Carthago to the Romans—posed the biggest threat to Rome. The Romans called the inhabitants of Carthage *Poeni*—the Latin word for Phoenicians and the origin of the English word "Punic." Carthage controlled a vast commercial empire that dominated trade in the central and western Mediterranean. Since Rome had no commercial or military fleet, the economic interests of Rome and Carthage had never come into conflict, so the two nations had peacefully coexisted for nearly two centuries.

When the Roman victory in the Samnite Wars brought the entire Italian peninsula south of the Po under Roman control, and with it the rich Greek cities of southern Italy that had been long-standing enemies of Carthage, the Carthaginians sensed a potential rival.

When both Carthage and Rome intervened in a dispute over control of a strategically placed city, relations became more complicated. Tensions between the two powers would explode into a total of forty-two years of war, which would destroy Carthage completely and forever alter the political, economic, and cultural life of Rome.

THE FIRST PUNIC WAR

The flash point for the rivalry between Rome and Carthage turned out to be the city of Messana (modern Messina) in northeastern Sicily. In 289 B.C., a band of Oscan mercenaries that had been discharged from the army of Agathocles, the tyrant of Syracuse, seized Messana, murdered the men, sold the children into slavery, and allotted the women among themselves. They called themselves Mamertines—sons of Mars in the Oscan language—and used Messana as a base for raids throughout northeastern Sicily. By 269 B.C., they were making forays into Syracusan territory, only to be defeated soundly by the Syracusan general, Hieron, who would later seize the throne of Syracuse as Hieron II.

Buoyed by this victory, Hieron, determined to end the Mamertines' reign of terror, attacked Messana itself. The Mamertines, faced with a disciplined attack and the certainty that Hieron planned to exterminate them in retribution for their vicious behavior, appealed to the Carthaginians for help. The Carthaginians, avid for Messana's strategic position on the strait between Sicily and Italy, sent a fleet and a small contingent of troops to aid the Mamertines. Faced with this increased opposition, Hieron withdrew his forces; however, the Mamertines' relief was short-lived because the Carthaginians refused to leave.

This time, the Mamertines resolved to appeal to Rome for aid in driving out the Carthaginians and to this end sent a delegation to the Roman Senate. The Senate heard the Mamertine ambassadors out and debated the issue, but as they were reluctant to make such an important decision without a broader consensus, they turned the problem over to the Comitia Centuriata. Seduced by visions of Messana's potential wealth, the citizen's assembly voted to send a small contingent of troops to Messana to help the Mamertines.

The War with Carthage and the Struggle
for the Western Mediterranean

Confronted with the Roman army, the Carthaginian commander lost his nerve, withdrew his forces, and returned to Carthage, where he was promptly crucified—the standard Carthaginian penalty for ineptitude.

With renewed determination to control Messana, the Carthaginians sent a new fleet with an army to Sicily. They also made an alliance with Hieron, arguing in their diplomatic mission to Syracuse that Rome's presence on the island of Sicily posed a threat to Syracuse. Together, the Carthaginians and the Syracusans advanced on Messana and sieged the Mamertines. Rome responded with reinforcements and, in 263 B.C., broke through the siege and pushed on to Syracuse, to which they in turn laid siege. At this point, Hieron had a change of heart and sued for peace, reasoning that, lacking a fleet, Rome could never really pose a serious danger to Syracuse, whereas Carthage, with its huge fleet and settlements in the west of Sicily, certainly could be. The Romans granted Hieron generous terms, confirmed his powers in southeastern Sicily, and thus won a firm ally who would stand by Rome until he died nearly forty-seven years later.

Carthage, however, now cut off completely from the east coast of Sicily by Hieron's defection, recruited an army and sent it to Agrigentum on Sicily's southwestern coast, intending to advance from there against either Syracuse or Messana. In June 262 B.C., however, the Romans preempted the Carthaginians by sending their own army west to Agrigentum to lay siege to the town. The city held out for six long months, during which time the Carthaginians sent another army to Sicily to attack the Romans from behind. With their superior manipular tactics, the Romans routed the Carthaginians on the battlefield outside the city, convincing the Punic garrison to abandon Agrigentum secretly at night; the following day, the Romans entered the town and sacked it.

The battle before Agrigentum taught the Carthaginians to respect the Roman army in the field, and they rarely challenged it again during the remaining nineteen years of the First Punic War. The reason for the military inequality between the two powers was simple: the Carthaginian army was composed of mercenaries fighting under Punic generals. Unless the general was especially inspiring and magnetic, the Carthaginian mercenaries could not be counted upon to fight with the same zeal as the citizen-soldiers of Rome.

THE WAR AT SEA

Unable to meet Rome on land in Sicily, the Carthaginians concentrated upon deploying their fleet. In direct contrast to their attitude toward their army, the Carthaginians lavished attention on their navy, for several reasons. The Carthaginians were originally Phoenicians, traditionally one of the great seafaring trading cultures of the Mediterranean; their navy was also the military muscle of their economy, protecting

Above: A Carthaginian breastplate shows a representation of Tanit, the Goddess of Fertility. Tanit was a North African goddess whom the Carthaginians adopted.

were powered by seventeen oars on either side manned by two rowers to each oar. The ships' sterns were decorated with a high curved sternpost that arced up and over the rear of the deck. The prow of each ship carried a seven-foot (2m) copper-covered ram just below the surface of the water that was designed not only to pierce the side of an enemy ship but also to break off so that the sinking enemy ship would not drag the attacking vessel down with it. The Carthaginian sailors prided themselves on the Punic vessels' great maneuverability: because they could wheel and turn quickly, ramming, rather than having soldiers boarding enemy vessels, was the main attack strategy.

Perhaps the most surprising discovery of the Marsala excavation was that the ships' keels and hulls were constructed with wooden beams fitted together without any wooden frames or ribbing such as modern ships have. Only afterward, when the keel and hull were finished, did the Carthaginian shipwrights add ribbing on the inside for support. Just as unexpected was the discovery in these ships of thousands of stems of *Cannabis sativa*, which would have been either chewed or brewed into a tea to lighten the burden of rowing.

The *liburnae* were small versions of the huge quinqueremes that formed the backbone of the Punic fleet. These ships carried crews of more than three hundred rowers, with five men assigned to each oar, and a small complement of marines. These were the ships that allowed Carthage to envision a war against Rome that entailed amphibious landings on the coast of Sicily behind Roman lines to cut off Roman armies from supply. At almost the same time, the Romans realized how vulnerable their armies were in Sicily without naval support and knew that they needed a fleet.

Above: A frieze from the Temple of Fortuna Primigenia (now in the Vatican Museum) depicts the type of Roman warship used during the Punic Wars. The long pole jutting out over the bow is a *corvus*, or raven, an iron beak designed to drop onto an enemy deck and hold the hostile ship next to the Roman vessel so soldiers such as these could jump on board and engage the enemy crew. The Romans sought to turn naval battles into infantry battles—the form of warfare in which they excelled.

a far-flung empire that extended from the shores of France, Spain, and Africa on the Atlantic to the coast of Libya and the islands of Sicily, Corsica, and Sardinia. Carthage employed the best naval architects and shipwrights from throughout the Mediterranean world and crewed the ships with Carthaginian citizens whose service aboard was mandatory, just as Roman citizens were required to serve in the army.

The Carthaginian fleet was kept in a high state of readiness and numbered about 120 of the powerful galleys known as quinqueremes, plus additional transport and reconnaissance vessels. A lucky find in 1969 allowed archaeologists to reconstruct a Punic warship. In that year, a sand dredge working off the coast of Marsala (ancient Lilybaeum) in western Sicily scooped up pieces of two ancient ships lying in only eight feet (2.5m) of water.

In 1971, archaeologists began excavating these vessels. Punic letters painted and scratched on parts of the hulls identified the ships as the small Carthaginian scout vessels that the Romans called *liburnae*, which

The War with Carthage and the Struggle
for the Western Mediterranean

ROME MEETS THE CHALLENGE

The Romans had neither ships nor the shipwrights to build them, but this did not prove a hindrance: when they found the wreck of a Punic quinquereme on the coast of Sicily, they quickly copied it. At the same time, they set about training crews by building rowing seats, or rums, on dry land and teaching soldiers to row in cadence and in unison.

Roman practicality added yet another dimension to their building and training program. The military knew they could never train crews in time to maneuver the huge ships as effectively as the Carthaginians did, with their years of naval practice and tradition behind them. The Romans simply decided not to compete with the Carthaginians on their terms, but to adopt a totally new tactic. They built long, narrow gangplanks about twenty-four by four feet (7.5 by 1.2m) mounted on swivels that were attached to the deck near the bow. These gangplanks each had, attached near the front on the underside, a long, sharp iron spike shaped like a raven's beak (the sailors called the whole apparatus a raven, or *corvus* in Latin). When a Roman ship got close enough to a Punic vessel, the Roman crew simply swung the raven out and dropped it on an enemy deck, where the beak embedded itself in the wood. This allowed the Roman infantry to rush across and onto the deck of the enemy ship, turning what was supposed to be a sea battle between sailors into a land battle between soldiers.

In order to utilize this new weapon effectively, the Romans added 120 marines to the crew of each warship.

In the spring of 260 B.C., the Roman consul Gaius Dullius led the new Roman fleet out to engage the Punic fleet off Mylae (modern Milazzo), a town on Sicily's northeast coast. The ravens took the Carthaginians completely by surprise, and in a short engagement the Romans captured fifty ships intact because the Punic crews were too dumbfounded to resist and probably lacked any infantry trained to resist the Roman boarders. The Carthaginians retreated in disorder, and Dullius returned to Rome as a hero to celebrate the first naval triumph in Roman history.

ON TO CARTHAGE

Emboldened by their victory, the Romans were determined to end the war by invading Africa and destroying the city of Carthage itself. In 256 B.C., the consuls Atilius Regulus and Manilius Vulso took twenty-five thousand troops to sea in a fleet of 330 quinqueremes and transports bound for the North African coast. The Carthaginians went to sea with two hundred quinqueremes, meeting the Romans off Cape Ecnomus on Sicily's southern coast. The Carthaginian strategy was to intentionally weaken the center of their own line in order to allow the Romans to break through. The Carthaginians put their main strength on the flanks so that as the Romans broke through the middle, the Punic vessels could sweep around to attack the Roman ships from behind.

The War with Carthage and the Struggle
for the Western Mediterranean

The ravens thwarted the Carthaginian strategy because the Roman vessels on the flanks held the Punic vessels stationary until the Romans' middle vessels could turn around and attack the Carthaginian vessels they had just broken through. When the battle was over, the Romans had lost twenty-four ships, but they had sunk thirty Punic vessels and captured sixty-four others. The Roman fleet sailed on to land their infantry, unopposed, on the African coast. In a short time, the Roman army had arrived within a day's march from Carthage.

The consul Manlius Vulso returned to Rome, leaving his fellow consul, Atilius Regulus, with fifteen thousand men to finish the task of defeating Carthage. Regulus had every reason to expect a Punic capitulation: their fleet was in ruins, their army was cowering behind the walls of Carthage, and the Punic population was panicking. Many felt that their plight was punishment for neglecting the gods, so to appease the deities they began a wholesale sacrifice of children to the god Baal Hammon and the goddess Tanit. These ceremonies took place in the infamous tophet, the circular open-air sanctuary south of the city.

Human sacrifice had fallen into disuse in much of the Mediterranean—the last official Roman instance of this practice took place in 288 B.C.—but the Carthaginians still sometimes practiced infant sacrifice. In times of danger to the state, the ruling class was expected to offer their own children for sacrifice. The infant was first strangled and then placed on the outstretched arms of one of two giant bronze statues, either Baal Hammon or Tanit. The statue's arms extended out over a circular fire pit—Cleitarchus of Alexandria, a third-century B.C. historian, recorded that the extreme heat caused the child's limbs to contract and the corners of the child's mouth to draw

back in a hideous grin, making the tiny corpse appear to be laughing. The priests then pushed the body into the flames, which soon reduced it to ashes; the ashes were later placed in large jars. A modern excavator at Carthage, Jeffrey Schwartz, carefully uncovered the remains of six hundred babies from the tophet site and found, through medical forensics, that while one-third were between the ages of two and three, the majority were one year old or younger.

Perhaps the fierce gods of Carthage heard this grisly prayer and sent a savior to Carthage in the form of Xanthippus of Lacedaemon, a mercenary captain who was able to train the normally unruly Carthaginian hired soldiers into an effective phalanx, lead them out to battle, and defeat Regulus and his army. The Carthaginians captured Regulus, but a few Roman survivors retreated to the coast, where they were rescued by a Roman relief fleet that was bringing reinforcements. The fleet set sail for Italy but on the way home sailed into a hurricane; of 330 warships and transports, 250 sank. Thus did a sequence of unforeseen disasters negate the equally astonishing Roman victories of the previous nine years.

From 255 to 241 B.C., the war between Carthage and Rome was confined to Sicily, where the Romans struggled to capture Panormus, Lilybaeum, and Drepana (modern Palermo, Marsala, and Trapani), the last Punic-controlled cities on the island. Although the effort was off to a good start when the Romans took Panormus in 250 B.C., it stalled before the gates of Lilybaeum and Drepana. In 249, half the Roman fleet that was trying to blockade Lilybaeum was destroyed by Carthaginian ships, while the other half sank in a storm. The Roman setback encouraged Carthage to negotiate an end to the war. They sent the captive consul, Atilius Regulus, back to Rome on parole to treat for peace, releasing him on the condition that he give his word of honor to return if he was unsuccessful. In true Roman style, however, Regulus went to Rome and argued *against* accepting the Punic offers of peace. When the Senate agreed with him and rejected the Carthaginian offer, Regulus honorably returned to Carthage, where he was seized by his angry captors, then sealed alive in a barrel pierced by dozens of long iron spikes that speared the consul when the Carthaginians rolled the barrel downhill.

The war continued for another eight years. Carthage sent a young aggressive commander, Hamilcar Barca, to Sicily to relieve the sieges of Lilybaeum and Drepana, but despite his brilliant efforts, Barca accomplished nothing in Sicily except to build within himself an intense hatred of everything Roman, which he would pass along, undiminished, to his son Hannibal.

In 242 B.C., the Romans taxed themselves heavily in order to finance a new fleet of two hundred quinqueremes, with which they cut off all supplies to Lilybaeum and Drepana, thereby forcing the cities to surrender. The capture of these two cities finally caused Carthage to accept defeat, and in 241 Carthage sued for peace, paying a a huge indemnity to Rome and ceding Sicily. The cost of the war and of the indemnity ruined Carthage economically, a situation made worse when the Punic mercenaries returning to Africa from Sicily mutinied upon learning that they would not be paid. The battle-weary Carthaginians went on to fight an internal war for two more years until the mutineers were defeated and crucified. When Rome took advantage of the Punic internal struggles to land troops on the Carthaginian possessions of Corsica and Sardinia, Carthage had no choice but to accept the situation.

THE OUTCOME

The First Punic War shifted the balance of power in the central Mediterranean to Rome. The Carthaginians had lost their supremacy at sea as well as their most profitable overseas possessions: Sicily, Corsica, and Sardinia. Yet Rome would not escape unscathed: by dictating such harsh terms to Carthage and then stealing Corsica and Sardinia from her at a time of helplessness, Rome created an unquenchable thirst for vengeance in this North African state—political forces in Carthage would demand another attempt to defeat the Romans. Rome still had her most demanding war ahead.

THE SECOND PUNIC WAR

The Carthaginians who most thirsted for revenge were members of the Barca family, a powerful and ancient clan that had the wealth and prestige to direct the city's foreign policy toward making Rome pay for her past actions. The head of the family, Hamilcar, looked forward to the day when he could again challenge Rome; for the time being, however, it was necessary to rebuild the fortunes of Carthage, and that would take time. Rome also needed time to recover from the costs of winning the war, and so for the next twenty-three years Rome and Carthage were at peace.

During that time, Rome turned her attention to the area north of the Po River, systematically conquering the Gauls, a Celtic people that for a century and a half had been staging attacks on southern Italy from there. In 225 B.C., Rome won a great victory against them at Telamon, on the Etruscan coast, and the Gauls grudgingly submitted. Yet they, too, harbored an intense hatred for the Romans and bided their time, awaiting an opportunity to revolt.

The War with Carthage and the Struggle
for the Western Mediterranean

The Carthaginians, meanwhile, were determined to rebuild the empire they had lost with Sicily, Sardinia, and Corsica by conquering Spain and exploiting its grain, silver, and tin. The Spanish adventure was Hamilcar's brainchild, and between 237 and 229 B.C. his personal energy and leadership created a new Punic empire in Spain. He was especially adept at dealing with the native Celts—a people related to the Gauls whom the Romans were subduing in northern Italy. The Celts were a proud, contentious, and habitually violent people whose society was dominated by blood feuds and endemic warfare, yet Hamilcar was able to win their respect and cooperation. When he died in 229, his son-in-law, Hasdrubal, continued his legacy, but upon Hasdrubal's death in 222, Hamilcar's son Hannibal assumed leadership in Spain.

The Roman historian Polybius, born some twenty years after Hasdrubal's death, tells a revealing story about Hannibal as a boy, which supports the Roman tradition that Hamilcar's goal in Spain was to build a base for his retaliation against Rome. In 238 B.C., when Hannibal was nine, his father took him to the Temple of Melgart, where he made the boy place his hand on the god's altar and swear eternal enmity to all Romans. When Hannibal assumed the leadership of Carthage's Spanish empire in 222, he remembered his boyhood oath and immediately began preparations for a bold and perilous scheme.

Hannibal's plan was audacious. He realized that Rome controlled the Mediterranean, so any attack utilizing sea power against Italy directly across the sea from Africa was bound to fail. The only alternative was to attack Rome by land, which meant leading troops out of Spain, across southern France, through the Alps, and down into the Po Valley of northern Italy. This would put a Punic army in the territory of the Italian Celts, kinsmen of the Spanish Celts whom Hasdrubal had persuaded to the Carthaginian cause and trained as expert and disciplined soldiers in the Punic phalanxes. It would be impossible, in the short time that he would have, to train the Italian Celts—still smarting from their defeat at Telamon—to be as disciplined soldiers as their Spanish cousins were, but what they lacked in training they might make up for in zeal and hatred toward the Romans.

Hannibal left his base, Cartagena, or New Carthage, in Spain in June 218 B.C.. His army numbered fifty thousand Celto-Spanish infantry men, nine thousand Numidian cavalrymen from North Africa, and thirty-seven elephants. Unfortunately, despite his best efforts at conciliation, some of the Celtic tribes in northern Spain and southern France had not been assimilated into the Carthaginian sphere and were suspicious of Hannibal's motives, believing that he really meant to conquer their land and add it to the Punic empire. As a result, Hannibal had to fight several battles on his way to Italy, but Punic training and discipline always won out against the wild battle madness of the Celts. Nevertheless, their opposition combined with losses due to cold, avalanches, and blizzards in the Alps cost Hannibal about twenty-three thousand men. All thirty-seven elephants survived the trip.

THE WAR IN ITALY

When Hannibal came down from the Alps with the remnants of his army, he began sixteen years of military campaigns throughout Italy; the battles he won during the first two years have inspired military leaders ever since. Always outnumbered, with half his army composed of poorly trained, undisciplined Gauls from northern Italy, and struggling with a makeshift supply system, Hannibal accomplished military miracles. In three major battles—at the Trebia River, in northwestern Italy; at Lake Trasimene, near Perugia; and at Cannae, near Barletta, in Bari province—Hannibal's army killed or captured 170,000 Romans and allied soldiers while losing only about a tenth of that number among his own troops.

These awesome results were not entirely the result of Hannibal's brilliance and good luck. To a large degree, the Roman losses in battle were due to poor leadership, if not downright stupidity, on the part of the Roman commanders. At the battles of Trebia River and Lake Trasimene, for example, the Roman leaders refused to use even the most rudimentary reconnaissance, so their armies were surprised and overwhelmed before the legions could deploy in their nearly impregnable manipular formations. At Cannae in June 216 B.C., the joint Roman command used troops who were inadequately trained in Roman warfare and who, lulled by the success of their initial attack, failed to realize that Hannibal had deceived them into a false sense of confidence. The result was one of the worst defeats in the history of Rome: fifty thousand Roman soldiers were killed and thirty thousand more surrendered. Ernlee Bradford, a modern biographer of Hannibal, claims that the fifty thousand Romans killed that day represent the largest number of troops felled in battle in a single day in all of history.

After this defeat, Rome should have opened negotiations with Hannibal. Instead, they just refused to quit. The Senate called for greater efforts on the part of all Roman citizens to supply troops and money. Most importantly—and surprisingly—Rome's allies, including many of the cities that had been conquered during the Samnite wars, stood firm in support of the Republic. Hannibal had expected these cities to rise up and regain their lost independence

The War with Carthage and the Struggle
for the Western Mediterranean

under his leadership, but almost none did. So fair and mild had Rome's treatment of these conquered cities been, and so prosperous had their economies become under Roman political domination, that few Italians saw any advantage in independence. The few cities that did defect to Hannibal, such as Capua and Tarentum, sent him not troops but only food and money.

Without reinforcements from the Italian allies, Hannibal soon had too few men to do anything but maintain himself in Italy. Time and again, he tried to lure a Roman army into new traps, but the Romans, refusing to fight him, simply retreated behind the walls of a nearby town and waited him out. Hannibal had no siege equipment with which to capture walled cities, so this was the perfect strategy to defeat him.

But it took so long! Rome began this tactic in 215 B.C., but Hannibal did not leave Italy for thirteen years. He marched back and forth from walled city to walled city, always hoping to draw the Romans out to where he could have beaten them in open battle. Having reached a stalemate in Italy, the war shifted to other theaters. Roman armies went to Spain, where,

Inventions of War

Archimedes (287–211 B.C.) was the most brilliant mathematician of the ancient world. Born in Syracuse, Archimedes was educated at Alexandria, Egypt, the center of science in the ancient world.

In Sicily, Carthage had recaptured the city of Agrigentum, lost in the First Punic War, and formed an alliance with the Greek city of Syracuse after Hieron, the pro-Roman ruler of that city, died in 215 B.C. Rome, despite the presence of Hannibal's troops all over Italy, dispatched an army under Claudius Marcellus to retake these two cities and thus drive the Carthaginians from the island. It took him four years to do so.

The Roman siege of Syracuse was made doubly difficult by the city's mighty walls and by the devices of the great Greek inventor Archimedes, who designed huge machines to defeat the Romans. His knowledge of mechanics allowed him to build catapults that outranged the Roman ones and huge cranes that either dropped great rocks on Roman warships or suddenly swung out over the city walls, dropped a grapple onto a Roman ship, hauled the vessel partway out of the water, and dropped it suddenly back into the water so that the impact broke the ship into segments. The Roman soldiers held Archimedes in such awe that they fled in panic whenever a wooden beam projected over the walls of Syracuse.

Finally, in 211 B.C., a traitor let the Romans into the city and the city fell, though Marcellus, desiring to exploit Archimedes' genius, gave strict orders that the Greek inventor was not to be harmed. A group of Roman soldiers discovered the scholar seated on a garden bench and oblivious to the noise and massacre going on in the city streets, so absorbed was he in scratching mathematical equations in the dirt. He either did not hear or refused to acknowledge a soldier's demand that he give his name. Enraged, the soldier killed Archimedes with a spear. The next year, disgruntled Carthaginian mercenaries betrayed Agrigentum to the Romans, and Sicily was once more firmly in Roman control.

despite serious defeats in 212 and 211 B.C., a recently promoted Roman commander, Publius Cornelius Scipio, known as Scipio Africanus the Elder, captured the Punic capital at Cartagena in 209 and razed two Carthaginian armies—one at Baecula in 208, the other at Ilipa in 206—leaving Spain firmly in Roman hands.

The Carthaginians tried twice to send supplies and reinforcements to Hannibal in Italy. In 207 B.C., Hannibal's brother Hasdrubal led an army of thirty thousand men along Hannibal's old route from Spain through the Alps into Italy. He reached northern Italy, recruited a number of Gauls to his cause, and began marching south to join Hannibal, who was in Lucania, at the southern end of the Italian peninsula. Unfortunately, the Romans intercepted Hasdrubal's letter to Hannibal and, using the information in it, the consul Gaius Claudius Nero won a complete victory over Hasdrubal near the Metaurus River on the central east coast of Italy. Hannibal learned of his brother's defeat when a Roman cavalry patrol threw Hasdrubal's head over the walls of the Carthaginian camp.

In 205 B.C., the Carthaginians tried once more to support Hannibal by sending his younger brother Mago to Liguria in northern Italy. Mago could not persuade the local Gauls to support him, and after two years of inconclusive fighting, he returned to Africa.

THE WAR IN AFRICA

By 205 B.C., however, the heart of the war had shifted to Africa. In that year, Publius Cornelius Scipio recruited two legions to invade Africa and landed the next year on the African coast near Utica, only a few miles north of Carthage. For two years, Scipio and the Carthaginians maneuvered and battled, each attempting

Above: In *Snow Storm: Hannibal and His Army Crossing the Alps*, Joseph Mallord William Turner (1775–1851)—renowned for his gift of abstract portrayal—captured the great danger and potential disaster that dogged Hannibal's route across the Alps into Italy, especially because he did not reach the western foot of the mountains until early fall.

The War with Carthage and the Struggle
for the Western Mediterranean

to recruit various North African chieftains to their cause. In 203, Scipio defeated the Carthaginians at the Battle of Bagradas (today Medjerda); the panicked Carthaginians finally called Hannibal home. Luckily for the Carthaginians, a Punic fleet sent to bring Hannibal and his troops out of Italy arrived at Crotona, on the "toe" of the Italian peninsula, without encountering the much larger Roman fleet. Hannibal and his fifteen thousand remaining troops sailed safely home to Africa, which Hannibal had last seen at the age of nine, forty-four years earlier, when he left for Spain with his father.

From this point, events moved quickly to converge at one last, epochal battle. Hannibal established his headquarters at Hadrumetum (today Sousse), ninety miles (145km) southeast of Carthage, while Scipio sent his troops into the rich farmland south of Carthage that supplied the city's food. On an unknown day in October 202 B.C. the two armies met in a final clash at Zama, a town about seventy miles (112.5km) southeast of Carthage. Hannibal knew that Scipio was much too clever a general to be tricked, so both sides drew their forces up in conventional battle lines, with the infantry in the center and small groups of cavalry on the flanks. Unfortunately for Hannibal, the Romans had recruited the young king Masinissa of Numidia to their cause and consequently had a much larger and better force of cavalry at their command than Hannibal.

Hannibal, for his part, was depending on eighty elephants—more than he had ever used in any battle. He planned to deploy them as the first line of his attack, sending them to disrupt the Roman infantry so badly that his own infantry could finish them off. The Romans had learned to fight elephants, however, and just before the great beasts reached the Roman front

ranks, the infantry shifted, allowing the elephants to pass. As the animals reached the rear, lightly armed spear carriers jabbed them in the side, causing them to panic; this in turn prevented their mahouts from turning them around. In the meantime, the Roman infantry closed ranks and advanced on the Punic infantry just as the Numidian cavalry swept out and around the Punic flanks to attack the Carthaginians from the rear. In a short time, the Carthaginian army was beaten and forced to surrender in the field. Carthage had no choice but to ask for terms.

The Romans were generous in victory. Carthage had to pay a huge indemnity of twelve hundred talents (a single talent equaled fifty pounds of silver), but had fifty years in which to do it. In addition, she had to surrender Spain to Rome, destroy all but ten warships, and return all prisoners of war and Roman deserters. It would not have been unheard of for Rome to ask for Hannibal as a hostage to hold for the good behavior of Carthage and to parade him in a triumphal procession through the streets of Rome and then execute him. The Romans did not do this because Scipio, out of his great respect for Hannibal, whom he had met briefly before the Battle of Zama, refused to see the Carthaginian general humiliated. Scipio also probably realized that only a leader of Hannibal's caliber could hold the Carthaginian state together and guarantee the payment of the indemnity.

Hannibal stayed in Carthage as a suffete, one of two chief magistrates of the city, for the next seven years. He reorganized the tax structure so that it was income-based, and thus more equitable, and rebuilt the Carthaginian trade network. So effective were Hannibal's reforms that Carthage was able to offer to pay off her indemnity forty years early. The sudden resurgence of wealth terrified the Roman Senate,

The War with Carthage and the Struggle
for the Western Mediterranean

HANNIBAL'S LAST YEARS

Hannibal did not wait to see what his countrymen would do. In 195 B.C., he set sail for Tyre, in what is today Lebanon, where he sought asylum with Antiochus. Whatever the truth of the Roman accusations before, once at the Seleucid king's court, Hannibal urged him to take on Rome; Antiochus did wage war, with Hannibal serving as the king's naval commander. When, in 189, the Romans finally defeated Antiochus, they demanded as a condition of peace that the king surrender Hannibal to them. Once more, Hannibal escaped, traveling to Crete, where he lived in obscurity at Gortyna, on the north coast near Knossos.

In 185 B.C., the Romans tracked him down, forcing him to flee once more. This time, he found refuge in

which feared a revival of Carthaginian military ambitions. Unwilling to risk the possibility, the Senate cooked up a false accusation against Hannibal: the Romans maintained that Hannibal had been corresponding with Antiochus III of Syria with an eye toward waging war on Rome once more and demanded that Carthage surrender their great leader.

Bithynia, on the north coast of modern Turkey, where King Prusias enlisted him in his war against neighboring Pergamum (today Bergama), an ally of Rome. In a naval battle between Bithynia and Pergamum, the catapults on the Bithynian ships threw clay jars full of poisonous snakes onto the decks of the enemy vessels, causing their crews to jump overboard. Unfortunately,

The War with Carthage and the Struggle
for the Western Mediterranean

the trick caught the attention of the Romans, who sent a force to Bithynia to demand that Hannibal be turned over to them. Prusias, unwilling to risk war with Rome, gave his permission. When the Romans arrived at Hannibal's villa at Libyssa, near Nicomedia (today Izmit), they found he had committed suicide—thus eluding them one last time.

THE CONQUEST OF GREECE

Carthage was not Rome's only adversary in the third century B.C. The political currents that influenced Romano-Punic relations also created a number of crises with the Greek states to the east.

Rome entered the Greek arena innocently enough when she dispatched two fleets in 229 and 221 B.C. to suppress pirates operating along the Illyrian coast of the Adriatic Sea. This activity aroused the suspicion of Philip V, king of Macedonia, who saw in Rome a

potential enemy. In reality, the Roman actions were intended purely to protect Italian and Roman merchants and their trade up and down Italy's Adriatic coast. Nevertheless, Philip felt threatened enough to form an alliance with Hannibal in 215 B.C. and to promise troops, although he never got around to sending any. This was no doubt because the Romans immediately sent a fleet to cruise the Macedonian coast, landing a small contingent at Apollonia, giving some of Philip's disgruntled subjects a group to rally around and be led by in a revolt.

To keep Philip honest and to discourage him from abetting Carthaginian designs, Rome also formed alliances with both the kingdom of Pergamum, in northwest Asia Minor, and with the Aetolian League, a confederation of small city-states in central Greece. A worried Philip signed a treaty with Rome in 205 B.C., thus ending the First Macedonian War, so-called by historians despite the lack of battles. None of Philip's actions so far had actually endangered Rome,

but they did make the Romans suspicious of the Macedonian ruler and judge him—correctly—as a potential threat to Roman commerce.

The tension between Rome and Macedon erupted into open war between 200 and 190 B.C., when Philip began to expand his kingdom into neighboring Greek states to the east. Fearing that this expansion would render Philip significantly more powerful, Rome reinforced its alliance with the Aetolian League and dispatched small contingents of Roman troops to Greece to participate in what became known as the Second and Third Macedonian Wars.

"GREECE FOR THE GREEKS"

The Roman hero of the Second Macedonian War was the general Titus Quinctius Flaminius. Flaminius had been quaestor in 199 B.C. and consul in 198; he was also an intellectual who, like many educated Romans, deeply admired Greek culture and spoke fluent Greek. He rallied the small Greek states to him by posing as the savior of Greek independence in the face of Macedonian tyranny. The master of what we today call the "sound bite," he devised a slogan—"Greece for the Greeks"—that made him a hero throughout the Greek peninsula. The allies he won made it possible for him in 197 to defeat Philip at the Battle of Cynoscephalae, in Thessaly in northeastern Greece. Soon after the battle, which decided the Second Macedonian War, Flaminius traveled to Corinth, where he dramatically announced to the Greeks that had assembled there for the Isthmian Games that the Roman Senate guaranteed the independence of Greece. Within three years, Rome had withdrawn all her soldiers from Greece.

Unfortunately, Rome was quickly drawn back into Greek politics when Antiochus III threatened, for reasons unrelated to Rome, to invade Thrace, in the eastern Balkan Peninsula, from his territory in Asia Minor. Antiochus had recently and successfully sent his army on a binge of conquest east to the Indus Valley and south to the Sinai, and considered it reasonable to add part of Greece to his empire. Rome feared that if this powerful ruler dominated Greece, he would be in a position to threaten Italy. In 192 B.C., therefore, they sent another army to Greece; made an alliance of convenience with their former enemy, Philip; and with him soundly thrashed Antiochus at Thermopylae in 191. The significance of a Roman victory on the same battlefield where Sparta had struggled against another Asian tyrant nearly three hundred years before was not lost on the Greeks, who again hailed Rome as the champion of Greek liberty.

The Romans chased Antiochus back to Asia Minor, where Scipio Africanus the Elder crushed him at the Battle of Magnesia (today Manisa). Despite their victory, the Romans were reluctant to govern a territory so far from Italy, and in 188, they negotiated a treaty with Antiochus. The would-be conqueror would cede all his possessions in northern Asia Minor to Rome's ally Pergamum, who had fought faithfully beside Rome. After the treaty was signed, Rome once more withdrew from Asia Minor and Greece, thus ending the Second Macedonian War.

Rome did not intervene again in Greek affairs for nearly twenty years. Philip's son Perseus, however, was as aggressive as his father, and in 171 B.C. he attempted to force all of Greece into a league under his leadership. The Romans, still fearing that such a political entity could challenge them in the Adriatic, sent an army to Macedonia, annihilating the Macedonian army at Pydna in 168 and capturing Perseus. Thus went the Third—and last—Macedonian War. Determined to break her adversary, Rome levied an enormous indemnity, carried away a large number of Macedonians as slaves, and dismantled the Macedonian kingdom into four small republics, each under native but pro-Roman leadership. To ensure good behavior, the Romans took one thousand hostages from among the first families of Macedonia and those Greek states that had willingly allied themselves with Perseus. Then, once more, they withdrew their armies.

This did not end matters with Greece. The Macedonians revolted against the puppet rulers in 150 B.C., and Rome sent yet another army to put the uprising down. This time, the Romans came to stay, made the territory a Roman province, and installed Roman garrisons. In response, the Achaean League, a federation of Greek cities, declared war on Rome. In 146 B.C., Rome dispatched another army.

By now Rome, weary of the troubles in Greece, was determined to make an example of her. Roman troops destroyed seventy of the most rebellious cities, including Corinth, and dragged 150,000 Greeks back to Rome as slaves. So thorough was Rome's "pacification" that Greece never again revolted.

THE FINAL CONQUEST OF CARTHAGE

At the same time that Rome was at war in Greece, she was also expanding westward. In addition, in 149 B.C., she intervened in a dispute between Carthage and Numidia, perhaps because of apprehension in the Senate that a possible Carthaginian triumph over Numidia would encourage a resurgence of military ambitions. Then again, the preemptive invasion could

merely have been an excuse to punish Carthage for past miseries that Carthage had inflicted on Rome.

The principal instigator of what was to be the Third Punic War was Marcus Porcius Cato, known as Cato the Censor. Born into a plebeian family, Cato's moral character initially won him many admirers. He held several offices and was a veteran of the Second Punic War and the Battle of Thermopylae; elected censor in 189, he imposed luxury taxes on women's fashionable dress and ornaments, vehicles, and slaves. Cato was a dangerous fanatic who cloaked his hatred and shortcomings in a fierce nostalgia for what he perceived to be the old customs and values of Rome. In some ways the ancient Roman equivalent of America's Joseph McCarthy, Cato saw a potential conspiracy in every action on the part of a foreign state and attacked his political enemies, including the Scipio family, on moral grounds.

While he hated Carthage because it might rival Rome, he also hated Greece because he feared that the temptations of soft Greek ways (for example, its traditional love of art) would feminize Rome, causing her to abandon her traditional virtues (the word is from the Latin *vir*, or "man"). Anyone who disagreed with him had to be guilty of impiety, treason, or dishonesty.

Carthage was at the top of his list of Rome's potential enemies, and so obsessive was Cato on the subject that whenever he spoke in the Senate—and he spoke often—no matter what the debate was on the Senate floor, be it taxes, sewers, Greek art, or noisy Roman streets, he closed with the same phrase: *"Carthago est delenda!"*—"Carthage must be destroyed!"

For whatever reason, in 149 B.C. the Senate accused Carthage of violating a technicality of the treaty signed after the Battle of Zama and laid down impossible conditions for peace, the most egregious being that the Carthaginians tear down their own city and move to a new site ten miles (16km) away from the sea. Well aware that this would mean economic suicide for a city that lived by trade, the Carthaginians refused to comply and began to plan for what they foresaw could be a futile war.

The siege of Carthage lasted three long years, chiefly because of the strength of the city's fortifications and the incompetence of the Roman commanders. Finally, in 147, the Romans appointed Scipio Aemilianus as commander; in less than a year he took the city by direct assault. The Romans poured over the walls from towers and ladders, and fierce fighting ensued in the streets for six days. Finally, the survivors surrendered, only to be sold as slaves. In 146, Scipio ordered the city razed, and some of the surrounding fields were sowed with salt, a symbolic gesture indicating that no crops would ever grow there again. The territory around Carthage was then organized into the new Roman province of Africa.

ROMAN EXPANSION IN THE IBERIAN PENINSULA

Roman expansion did not stop with Greece and Carthage. The 140s also saw the beginning of a long war in Spain and Portugal for complete control of the Iberian peninsula. The Romans had inherited Carthaginian Spain, that is, the eastern and southern areas of the peninsula, but now they wanted it all, in part because of constant raids by the Celtic Iberians who lived in the north and west of the peninsula and in part because of rumors that the interior held rich silver and gold mines.

Both the geography and the character of the inhabitants made conquest difficult. Its mountainous interior, which was slashed with numerous valleys, impeded travel, especially for large armies, while at the same time keeping the native population divided into small, autonomous tribes. There was no centralized government to surrender—Rome would have to defeat each tribe separately.

The Iberian tribes fielded gifted military leaders who waged a series of long and successful guerrilla wars against Rome based upon a strategy of swift strikes, followed by equally swift retreats into the inaccessible mountain vastnesses of the interior. One leader in particular, Viriatus, a shepherd, carried on a brilliant campaign against Rome in the western part of the Iberian peninsula, now the border between Portugal and Spain. In 141 B.C., Viriatus trapped a Roman army of fifty thousand men and parlayed their release into a treaty with Rome, by which the Republic agreed to respect the independence of his tribe. Barely a year later, the Romans arranged to have Viriatus assassinated and subjugated his homeland.

This act of treachery inspired the Iberian tribes to unite, and the war dragged on for another ten years. The Romans gradually won by bribing some of the tribes to take arms against their kinsmen and by wholesale slaughter, enslavement, or deportation of others. The Iberian war was one of the most ignoble in Roman history—the brutality of the Romans has been compared to U.S. policy in Vietnam and Soviet policy in Afghanistan. By 134 B.C., Scipio Aemilianus had driven the last group of Iberian resistance fighters into Numantia, a hilltop fortress in north central Spain, and starved them into surrender. That surrender would put an end to resistance in the Iberian peninsula for nearly a century.

CHAPTER V

Changes in
Roman Society

༄

202-80 B.C.

Pages 82–83: The House of the Vestal Virgins was a circular marble building in which vestal virgins·tended a sacred fire that was never allowed to die. The temple also contained the Palladium, a wooden statue of Athena supposedly brought to Rome by Aeneas, and a statue of a large phallus that the Romans believed was a charm against evil.

NEARLY 130 YEARS OF fighting in Italy and abroad created tensions in the fabric of Roman society that would change the Roman people and their institutions forever. During the war years, the Senate had gradually taken the reins of government out of the hands of the various Comitiae, or people's assemblies. Economically, the thousands of peasant farmers who during the Second Punic War had taken refuge in the city of Rome from waves of marauders—the Carthaginian army, mercenaries from both sides, and assorted brigands—now found themselves with few resources to support them. Militarily, the war transformed the Roman army from a part-time militia made up of farmers to a full-time professional field force. These changes, taken together, would ultimately destroy the republican form of government and give rise instead to a dictatorial government headed by an emperor.

THE RISE OF SENATORIAL POWER

Rome had had a Senate since the days of the kings, but before the Punic wars and the foreign wars in Spain, Greece, and Asia Minor, the Senate had shared the government of Rome with three citizen assemblies: the Comitia Tributa, the Comitia Curiata, and the Comitia Centuriata. Rome's initial military action in the First Punic War—sending troops to defend Messana from the Carthaginians—was a decision reached jointly by the Comitia Centuriata and the Senate.

As the war against Carthage dragged on, however, the need to act quickly was perceived as outweighing the need for a genuine consensus on the part of the citizen assemblies. The Senate, with its cohesive membership of three hundred, began to direct the war. Throughout the third century B.C. and into the second, the Senate directed Rome's military, financial, legal, and foreign affairs—while preserving the legal fiction of passing all decisions along to the popular assemblies, which merely rubber-stamped the Senatorial decrees.

The Senate in turn was controlled at any one time by some fifteen to twenty families, making Rome, in effect, an oligarchy. By this time the old division between the patricians and the plebeians had failed to mean anything. Some families, like the Cornelii, Aemilii, Claudii, Valerii, and Fabii, had been senatorial since Rome was a kingdom. Other families were of more recent origin but no less proud and protective of their Senate status. For other families, membership depended almost entirely upon sponsorship by one of the current families in the Senate, which enacted a series of laws intended to protect its power. First, a member had to hold land worth at least 400,000 sesterces, a huge sum. Then, no one could become a senator unless he had previously held office as a quaestor, an office that had financial and/or judicial functions. Although the quaestorship was an elected position, it was virtually impossible for a man to be elected to any political office in Rome without the support of at least some of the senatorial families.

Even the tribunes, who collectively had enough power to block senatorial legislation, ceased to exercise this power during the Punic wars; instead, their role became to persuade the plebeians in the popular assemblies to accept the decrees of the Senate. Thus, by the end of the Second Punic War, the Roman government was firmly under the control of the three hundred senators, who, like all such bodies before or since, tended to protect their financial and political interests at the expense of the Republic.

THE SECOND PUNIC WAR AND THE ECONOMY OF ROME

The economic forces that the Punic wars unleashed—largely the consequences of the Punic army's roaming the length of Italy, uprooting thousands of rural families, and driving them into the city of Rome—were as radical as the political changes during this period. In some cases, these rural families were forced to leave their farms behind because the major cultivator of the farm was absent for years at a time while serving in the army.

During the Punic wars, the population of Rome ballooned from a relatively small number of citizens (those born or freed in the city) to nearly 250,000. This massive influx of people found employment on the lowest levels of the Roman economic sector, often working in the factories and other businesses that supported the war effort. These workers lived in poorly constructed, unstable, combustible apartment houses called *insulae* ("islands").

A great many were hired on as rowers aboard Rome's great ships; contrary to the modern opinion spawned by the movie *Ben Hur*, Roman warships were not powered by galley slaves. Most of the immigrants from the country lived hand-to-mouth, making them vulnerable to exploitation by the rich and influential. At election time, the enfranchised poorest sold all they had—their votes or approval of Senate measures in the popular assemblies—for grain or money.

Between periods of fighting, the population of Rome was further swollen by discharged soldiers,

Below: Fighting gladiators adorn a circus scene mosaic in the Gallery Borghese in Rome. Romans learned about gladiators from the Etruscans, who traditionally staged gladiator fights as part of funerals. Gladiators were usually slaves and war captives, but a few were free men who volunteered to fight for the promise of excitement and prize money.

who often returned home to find their farms in ruin. Many of these men also moved to Rome looking for work. The problems of overpopulation in Rome were compounded by periodic grain shortages and inflation, which sometimes put prices beyond people's ability to pay. The wealthy, realizing the potential political dangers that the increasing economic tensions posed, relieved much widespread misery with qualified "charity" and sought to appease the discontented, often desperate populace with public baths and spectacular public entertainments. (Still today, the phrase "bread and circuses," borrowed from Juvenal, a satirist under the Empire,

describes measures taken by a government to appease discontent aroused by severe economic conditions.) The most popular of these spectacles were, of course, gladiatorial combats and beast fights between wild animals and professional hunters. These events, comparatively rare in the immediate postwar period, never failed to entertain and to garner votes.

The population surges into Rome resulted in another serious economic transformation: the creation of huge agricultural estates, the *latifundia*, at the expense of the small landowners. Once Hannibal had been driven from Italy, wealthy individuals found they could buy, at very low prices, the abandoned or collateralized farms of the Roman and Italian peasants who had had to abandon them while serving in the army. The wealthy were also able to buy land taken from the few disloyal Italian cities, such as Tarentum and Capua, who had supported Hannibal.

The huge migration from the farms to Rome weakened the Roman army by reducing the number of potential recruits, since Roman law decreed that only landowners could serve. Ironically, that law,

Changes in Roman Society

which created an army made up principally of small peasant landowners, ultimately dispossessed many of those landowners by sending them to fight far from home for years at a time, during which time their farms lay fallow and unproductive. With the manpower away fighting, the wife and children had to move; they usually traveled to Rome to live with relatives. Once discharged from the army, the farmers had little hope of wringing a living from their land; once they abandoned their farms to move to Rome, they and their children would be forever ineligible to serve, and thus unable to fulfill the obligation of a citizen outside Rome. And indeed, by 150 B.C., army recruiters were finding it difficult to conscript enough eligible men into the legions.

DANGEROUS REFORMS: TIBERIUS SEMPRONIUS GRACCHUS

The unsoundness of a system that deprived solid Roman citizens of their livelihood, corrupted the Republic's political traditions, decreased the number of men in the army, and encouraged slave revolts did not escape the notice of some Romans. One of them, Tiberius Sempronius Gracchus (163–133 B.C.), the grandson of Scipio Africanus the elder, decided to remedy the problem when he won election as tribune in 133 B.C.. As soon as he assumed office, he proposed an agrarian reform that he believed would send Romans streaming back to the countryside to work their farms and, in the process, save the Republic.

Tiberius proposed breaking up the great latifundia into small plots of about fifteen *iugera* (about nine acres [3.5ha]) and giving one to every dispossessed Roman male. Technically, this would have been easy to do since Roman law forbade anyone to hold a single piece of farmland larger than five hundred iugera (about three hundred acres [120ha]). This law had been quietly ignored for years by the wealthy Romans who owned the latifundia, property that could amount to thousands of iugera; as Tiberius explained to the Concilium Plebis Tributa, the government had been allowing the city's rulers to break the law. He argued that his proposal would merely reinstate an existing law, but that the Romans would thereby reclaim their peasant heritage and become eligible to serve in the army again, while the urban population of Rome would decrease. The repopulation of the countryside would also put an appreciable number of free citizens in a position to control the agricultural slave population. Tiberius even suggested funding the cost of tools and seed from the public treasury, recently swollen by the legacy of Attalus III, king of Pergamum, who died that same year, 133, willing his country and its treasury to the Roman Republic.

The wealthy landowners—many of them senators—were naturally enraged; to protect their holdings, they persuaded Tiberius' fellow tribune, Marcus Octavius, to veto the proposed bill. Tiberius countered Octavius' constitutionally sound action with one that was constitutionally questionable. He went before the Concilium Plebis Tributa and demanded that they remove Octavius from office, arguing that Octavius' veto showed that he no longer had the interests of the people at heart. The Concilium Plebis Tributa agreed, stripped Octavius of his office, and voted to enact Tiberius' reforms. The law included a provision to establish a land commission to oversee the distribution of the land and the breakup of the latifundia: Tiberius appointed himself, his brother Gaius Sempronius Gracchus, and his father-in-law, Appius Claudius, to serve on the commission.

That was not the end of the opposition to the new law, however. Tiberius had neglected to inform the Senate before submitting his law to the Concilium Plebis Tributa, and though technically he was not obliged to, the practice had become so established throughout the period of the Punic wars that it now seemed illegal. Perhaps Tiberius neglected to present his bill before the Senate because he knew the reception it would get; perhaps he was a true revolutionary seeking to restore to the Concilium Plebis Tributa the power he felt they never should have surrendered to the Senate. In any event, his exclusion of the Senate from the legislative process only intensified the senators' antagonism.

The Senate became determined to stop Tiberius at any cost; an opportunity presented itself when Tiberius ran for tribune a second time. The Roman constitution neither explicitly forbade nor sanctioned this; ancient custom alone prevented a tribune from immediately running for reelection after his first term. Still, the unorthodoxy of Tiberius' move provided the Senate with a chance to whip up public sentiment against him—to no avail. When it looked as if Tiberius would win the election anyway, the Senate, led by one of the consuls, Scipio Nasica, gathered a mob of sympathizers and slaves who armed themselves with wooden legs torn from benches and tables, marched to the Forum—where the vote was taking place—and there beat Tiberius and three hundred of his supporters to death. The mob gathered up the bodies and dumped them into the Tiber. The next day, the newly elected consul, Popillius Laenas, authorized a special court to arrest and try any followers of Tiberius who had escaped the previous day's slaughter. Ironically, had the senators waited for the final vote count, they would have been rid of Tiberius legally, for he failed to win the election by a narrow margin.

What had happened, however, was the most devastating event in the history of the Republic, and it set the Republic on the course that would ultimately destroy it. By resorting to violence, the Senate—a legally constituted entity—had, in a day, annihilated all constitutional safeguards against tyranny. It was as if the president of the United States were to encourage a mob of his supporters to march to the Capitol armed with clubs, enter the House or Senate chamber, and beat to death the leader of the opposition party and his followers. The Roman Senate had committed a previously inconceivable crime, ushering in nearly ninety years of class warfare, massacre, and general anarchy.

Oddly enough, the Senate allowed the newly enacted land law and its land commission to stand. The commission, minus Tiberius but with his brother Gaius, started its work of taking land away from some of the latifundia and redistributing it to Roman citizens. Ultimately, it would resettle seventy thousand of the urban poor onto new farms and create the pool of potential soldiers that Tiberius had envisioned.

We can only speculate about why the Senate killed the sponsor of a new law they hated and yet allowed the program that the law created to stand. Perhaps they were shocked and awed by what they had done, and thankful that the Roman people had not retaliated and killed them in turn, or they may have feared that if they did not institute this reform, somebody in the Gracchan party might lead a similar attack on them.

In any case, violence was now part of Roman politics. In 131 B.C., the tribunes were forced to intervene when one of their number, Gaius Atinus, lost his temper with the censor, Mettelus Macedonicus, and tried to throw him off the Tarpeian Rock at the back of the Capitoline. In 129, Scipio Aemilianus, the general who had sacked Carthage, was murdered in his bed the night before he was to propose land reforms benefiting Rome's Latin allies.

POLITICS WITH A VENGEANCE: GAIUS SEMPRONIUS GRACCHUS

In 123 B.C., Tiberius' brother, Gaius Sempronius Gracchus, won election as a tribune. For the ten years since his elder brother's death, he had been nursing his hatred of the Senate as a quaestor in Sardinia and was therefore not in Rome to pursue politics. Now he meant not only to obtain vengeance but to do it legally. The Roman citizens, beneficiaries of his martyred brother's policies, were willing to pass whatever legislation Gaius proposed out of respect for Tiberius' memory.

In 131 B.C., the Concilium Plebis Tributa passed a law that allowed for secret ballots; in 129, they passed one that allowed a tribune to hold consecutive terms. No longer could the Senate intimidate voters at the polls by watching for whom they voted. The Gracchi brothers' laws were revolutionary, and all of them were aimed to weaken the Senate one way or another and to build a power base in the people's assemblies: banishment was the automatic penalty for anyone who killed a Roman citizen (as soon as it passed, Scipio Nasica, the consul who had led the attack on Tiberius, was exiled); Tiberius' land reform act was extended; people other than senators were eligible to be governors of provinces; a special criminal court staffed by members of the *equites*, the Roman middle class, was empowered to investigate charges of criminal acts by senators; and to help feed the urban poor, the state imported grain from Sicily and Sardinia, stored it in government warehouses at Ostia, and sold it to Roman citizens below cost and at a fixed price.

As with his brother, the Senate had to accept Gaius' popularity and laws for a time, but in 121 B.C. they stirred up popular opposition to him by accusing him of impiety. Fearing attack, his followers panicked and barricaded themselves on the Aventine. The Senate, declaring this an illegal act and an attack on the state, voted an emergency measure, the *Senatus Consultum Ultimum*, authorizing the use of force. They sent a contingent of mercenary archers to attack the Aventine fortifications; between the initial assault and subsequent

Below: Romans seldom grew olives as a single crop because the trees took too long to bear fruit, and the crop varied so much from year to year. Olives were harvested in autumn and winter, times that the Romans felt ensured a good-quality oil.

executions, three thousand of Gaius' followers died. Gaius himself escaped execution by committing suicide. A reign of terror followed Gaius' death—his supporters were hunted down and Tiberius' land reforms were repealed. The Senate passed laws allowing themselves and other wealthy Romans to add new lands to their latifundia.

GAIUS MARIUS

After the death of Gaius Gracchus, the Senate felt itself securely in control of the government. Unfortunately, the senators did not subsequently govern well, and the Roman citizens, having tasted power under the Gracchus brothers, became discontented. The people found a champion in a rough, unsophisticated soldier named Gaius Marius (157–86 B.C.), who was able to capitalize on the political scandals and military defeats that followed the demise of Gaius Gracchus.

In 114 B.C., a Roman army under Marcus Porcius Cato, the grandson of Cato the Censor, was defeated by the Scordisci, a Celtic tribe living just over the border from Roman Macedonia. A year later, the Cimbri and the Tuetones, two Germanic tribes, defeated a Roman army just north of the border of Roman Italy. The panic that seized escalated when a Vestal was killed by lightning. Believing the gods to be against Rome, the people demanded human sacrifices to appease them; a Greek man and woman and a Gallic man and woman were buried alive.

At the same time, Rome was facing trouble in the North African kingdom of Numidia, an ally of Rome since the final war against Carthage. In 118 B.C., civil war broke out in Numidia; the victor, Jugurtha, a brilliant but brutal leader, claimed victory after a protracted siege of Cirta, the Numidian capital, in 112. When Jugurtha took Certa, he massacred Roman citizens who were part of a trading colony there, which so angered the Roman people that they demanded that the Senate declare war against Jugurtha.

A military fiasco of the first magnitude followed. The first war ended in 111 B.C., when Lucius Calpurnius

Bestia was apparently bribed by Jugurtha to make peace; the second ended in 109, when the army led by Spurius Postumius Albinus was trapped and forced to surrender in a humiliating ceremony wherein each man had to pass under a yoke, recalling the Samnite defeat of the Roman army at the Caudine Forks two centuries earlier. A new army was sent to Africa under Quintus Caecilius Metellus, who conducted a successful campaign but failed to defeat Jugurtha decisively. When the Romans demanded an explanation, a tribune, Gaius Mamilius, persuaded the Concilium Plebis Tributa to authorize a formal investigation, which revealed a long history of senatorial incompetence, poor decisions, and, worst of all, evidence that senators had accepted bribes from Jugurtha during the war. A number of senators were exiled, and the people demanded a new consul. In 107, the choice fell upon Gaius Marius.

The Roman populace liked Marius, who was not of the senatorial class but the son of a successful middle-class farmer from the northern Italian town of Arpinum. His appearance matched his origins: he was short and rough-looking, with a fierce gaze. Proud of his peasant origins, he mistrusted culture and openly criticized the practice of the educated Roman classes of speaking Greek rather than their own practical, basic Latin. His popularity rose from his successful military career as well—he had fought with distinction in Spain and later in Africa, where he had been an able subordinate.

Marius' reforms of the army allowed him to achieve spectacular results on the battlefield. In 107 B.C.,

Marius' Military Reforms

Gaius Marius realized that the Roman army needed drastic reforms, beginning with rigorous training and discipline. He required his soldiers to go on long fatigue marches, dig ditches, carry heavy loads, and undergo hours of sword practice. In the meantime, he completely reorganized the legions, raising the number of heavy infantry troops in a legion to six thousand and replacing the manipulus with a larger new tactical unit, the cohort, which contained six hundred men. To build unit pride, he introduced the silver eagle standard as the symbol of each legion. He even redesigned the pilum, the long spear that each soldier carried into battle, to make the weapon impractical for the enemy to pick up and throw back but reparable after a battle, when time permitted.

Marius' most far-reaching innovation, however, was his recruitment of soldiers from among citizens who did not own property. He required only that they be physically fit, and his offer of regular pay and a grant of land after twenty years in the army proved very attractive to the unemployed urban poor, and Rome soon had a full-time, regular army.

The soldier on the left is a standard bearer for his cohort. The round object at the top of his staff is a victory crown that the unit won for bravery in action. The other soldier is a regular legionnaire on the march with a typically rectangular curved shield, a helmet, and a pilum (spear) over his shoulder, and what appears to be a chicken (perhaps dinner) clutched in his hand.

the troops he led to Numidia defeated Jugurtha's armies in a series of lightning strikes. His capable assistant, Lucius Cornelius Sulla, captured Jugurtha himself, who was obliged to parade in royal robes before Marius' triumphal chariot. After the ceremony, Jugurtha was strangled in the Tullianum prison.

Hard on the heels of Marius' African success were his victories in Europe, where the Cimbri, the Tuetones, and another Germanic tribe, the Ambrones, were threatening Roman possessions in southern Gaul and northern Italy. As his price for leading the armies, Marius demanded immediate reelection as consul, which meant waiving the mandatory ten-year waiting period between terms. Following his reelection in 104 B.C., he defeated the barbarians first at the Battle of Aquae Sextiae in 102 and then, decisively, at the Battle of Vercellae in 101. Between both battles, he is supposed to have killed or captured 100,000 Germans.

Marius returned to Rome in triumph—just in time to deal with a crisis that was not directly military. The Senate, as jealous of its power as ever, was embroiled in a struggle with a tribune named Lucius Appuleius Saturninus, who had passed a number of laws that interfered with a senator's ability to accumulate land and appeared to give some recently conquered land to non-Roman allies.

Marius was sympathetic to Saturninus' laws, but the Senate, hoping to make trouble for the powerful Marius, ordered him to arrest Saturninus on a trumped-up charge of treason. Marius did so, but locked Saturninus and his followers in the Senate building for their own protection. A mob, urged on by the Senate, climbed onto the roof, tore up the roofing tiles, and pelted Saturninus and his followers to death with the tiles. Marius, fearing for his life, left for the eastern Mediterranean until the political climate cooled in Rome.

Changes in Roman Society

LIVIUS DRUSUS AND THE SOCIAL WAR

If the senators had hoped that things would improve for them with Marius out of the way, they were mistaken. In Marius' wake, a new political reformer emerged: Livius Drusus was an idealist who sought to end the violence of Roman politics, but his efforts only exacerbated matters. Intending to make the Senate more responsive, he proposed doubling its membership by admitting the equites, but the senators refused to share their power with social inferiors. At first, Drusus' popularity with the urban mob—a result of his support of lower grain prices—protected him from the Senate. A few months later, however, when Drusus proposed extending citizenship rights to Rome's Italian allies, the senators were able to whip up lower-class opposition to him since the urban poor believed that expanded citizenship rights, including the right to vote, would dilute their power in the various assemblies. On the other hand, the Italian allies, who had been supplying half the manpower for the Roman legions since the First Punic War, felt entitled to full citizenship. An alliance between the Senate and the urban poor frustrated Drusus' every attempt to win his program. Finally, Drusus was assassinated outside his home by an unknown assailant.

Drusus' murder angered the Italian allies, who, with their champion dead, declared their independence from Rome. The spark that ignited this radical move came in 90 B.C., when the Roman praetor, Gaius Servilius Caepio, delivered a speech to the Italian allies of the city of Asculum that disparaged their request for citizenship. A mob rushed the speaker's platform and beat him to death; they then hunted down and slaughtered every Roman citizen in Asculum. The revolt spread south all the way to the "toe" of Italy. Only Umbria, Etruria, Campania, and the major coastal cities that already had Roman citizenship stayed with Rome.

The Italian allies, quickly organizing their own armies, established a political structure for their new country, which they called Italia. They made Corfinium, only seventy-six miles (122km) from Rome, the capital, instituted a senate, and elected two consuls. They struck their own coins—some of which bore the image of an Italian bull goring a Roman wolf. Veterans of Rome's many wars peopled Italia's army, and two experienced generals, Quintus Pompaedius Silo and Gaius Papius Mutilus, commanded it.

In Rome, the senators panicked, realizing that even though they had mistrusted him, Marius was their most capable general. They recalled him from the east, but still wary, they made him second in command under two inferior generals, Publius Rutulius Lupus and Quintus Servilius Caepio, who performed incompetently and died in two battles of the war. Both these battles would have been catastrophic defeats had Marius not assumed command, saving the remnants of the two armies.

The Social War dragged on for two years until the Roman Senate realized that it would be too costly to defeat the allies militarily. After all, the allied armies were trained soldiers, who more than matched the Romans' skill and training. In 88 B.C., Lucius Julius Caesar (a distant cousin of Julius Caesar) persuaded the Senate to offer the allies full citizenship, and the rebellion began to collapse. Most of the allied cities made peace with Rome, but Asculum held out. The Roman army took the city by storm, massacred the garrison, and sold the population into slavery in retaliation for the murder of so many Roman citizens two years before.

LUCIUS CORNELIUS SULLA

Unfortunately, the peace did not end the violence that was now endemic to every level of the political process in Rome. When Sulpicius Rufus, a tribune, tried to gain command of a Roman army in Asia Minor for Marius, Lucius Cornelius Sulla, who sought command of that army for himself, unleashed a group of his followers to riot on his behalf. When his thugs were beaten up by a group loyal to Marius, Sulla fled for protection to—of all people—Marius, who, honoring the rules of hospitality, gave him sanctuary. Sulla subsequently escaped from the city, gathered troops, and brought an army into Rome itself, something hitherto unthinkable. But no longer: from this point on, the use of the army in politics became a Roman institution.

Sulla turned out to be a monster. He arrested Marius' supporter Sulpicius Rufus, had him murdered, and stuck his severed head on the rostrum, the speaker's platform in the Forum. He ordered the arrest of Marius, who was fleeing toward the coast. When Marius was arrested near Minturnae, on the west coast of Italy, Sulla sent orders for his immediate execution. But when the slave sent to execute him entered his cell with an ax, Marius arrogantly asked him if he had come to kill the savior of the Republic; the slave, abashed, refused to kill him and fled the prison. When the officials at Minturnae heard of the dramatic incident, they released Marius, who fled to the eastern end of the Mediterranean to raise his own army.

Sulla now turned to restoring the dominance of the Senate. He transferred the power of the Concilium Plebis Tributa to the Comitia Centuriata, where the voting procedure favored the wealthy classes most likely to support the Senate's programs. He

also pushed through a law that required all consuls and tribunes to submit proposed legislation to the Senate for approval.

Having successfully driven out Marius and shored up the power of the Senate, Sulla had himself appointed to military command and in 87 B.C. left for Asia Minor to carry on a war against Mithridates VI (120–63 B.C.), king of Pontus, on the north shore of Asia Minor. During the war against the allies, Mithridates had invaded Greece and captured Athens, perhaps hoping to move on to an invasion of Italy. Sulla landed an army in Greece, chased Mithridates back to Asia Minor, and forced him to sign a treaty with Rome.

Sulla then quickly embarked his army for Italy, for no sooner had he left to fight Mithridates than Marius returned to Italy with his own army, bent on capturing Rome. This was a different Marius than the one who had left Italy earlier; perhaps he had suffered a mental breakdown as a result of his treatment at the hands of Sulla and the Senate, for upon his return to power he unleashed a brutal reign of terror on the city. He undertook a wholesale massacre of the senators, their families, and their followers. Senators' heads, set on sharpened stakes, now decorated the main streets of Rome and the rostrum in the Forum, while the headless torsos were left unburied in the streets. Gangs of slaves and lower-class Romans broke

Above: Marcus Licinius Crassus (100?–53 B.C.) was a supporter of Sulla who made a fortune during Sulla's rule in Rome by buying at bargain prices the property of the men Sulla executed. After Sulla's death, Crassus became an ally of Caesar, and with Pompey formed the First Triumvirate.

Changes in Roman Society

Right: The tomb of Caecilia Metella—daughter of Metellus Creticus and wife to Caesar's rival Marcus Lucinius Crassus—was the largest along the Appian Way. The circular building in the background on the left is the tomb of the emperor Hadrian, built in A.D. 138. In the Middle Ages the popes fortified the building and used it for a fortress, the Castel Sant' Angelo.

into the homes of the rich and looted at will. Marius repealed all of Sulla's legislation and engineered his own election as consul—his seventh term. Then, at the height of his power, Marius suffered a massive stroke and died.

THE DEFEAT OF MARIUS

While Marius ruled, Sulla had been finishing the war against Mithridates. In May 83 B.C., vastly enriched by the tribute that Mithridates had paid, Sulla returned to Italy, fought a whirlwind campaign against Marius' son, also named Gaius Marius, and defeated and killed him. Now master of Rome, he gave himself up to an orgy of killing Marius' supporters.

Revenge motivated the executions in part, but economics also played a role because Sulla confiscated the property of his victims and divided it among the army and his own faction. Looking outside Rome, he confiscated the lands of cities and towns that had remained loyal to Marius and drove thousands of

farmers into the mountains, where they were reduced to banditry.

Sulla used his plunder to entrench the authority of the Senate. To facilitate this, he had the Comitia Centuriata grant him absolute dictatorial power for an indefinite period. Next, he increased the number of senators by allowing two hundred of the richest equites to become senators. (Although the Senate had been against this move when it was proposed by Drusus, Sulla was in a much more powerful position.) He abolished the popular courts, replacing them with courts over which senators presided, and forbade the tribunes to intervene on questions and laws of the Senate.

In 80 B.C., after being elected consul, he oversaw his new government for a year, convinced that by restoring the ancient power of the Senate he was returning Rome to a blissful golden age under the aegis of the aristocracy. He retired to private life but died in 79 B.C. of a stroke within the year; shortly after, his carefully—and brutally—crafted government began to fall apart.

Changes in Roman Society

THE UNHOLY ALLIANCE

Civil war broke out immediately between two of Sulla's subordinates, Marcus Aemilius Lepidus and Gnaeus Pompeius Magnus (better known as Pompey the Great). Pompey defeated Lepidus only to be faced with another contestant, Quintus Sertorius, a brilliant general who controlled the Roman army in Spain. Unable to defeat Sertorius militarily, Pompey had him assassinated.

In Asia Minor, Mithridates VI seized his opportunity, with Pompey engaged in Italy and Spain, to attempt to win back what he had lost to Sulla in 83 B.C. By 67, however, Pompey was victorious in western Asia as well, having conquered Asia Minor and Syria. He had also accumulated a huge fortune from his conquests, part of which he used to give each soldier a bonus equal to twelve years' pay.

While Pompey was fighting in Asia, the situation was deteriorating in Italy. Beginning in 73 B.C., a slave army, led by the famed Spartacus, annihilated nine Roman armies, terrifying Italy from 73 until 71, when a praetor, Marcus Licinius Crassus, known as "the Rich," trapped him and killed more than sixty thousand of his followers. To celebrate his victory and post a warning, Crassus lined the one hundred miles (161km) of the Appian Way from Capua to Rome with six thousand crucified slaves. A former ally of Sulla, Crassus, like Pompey, was wealthy, having speculated successfully in confiscated property during Sulla's regime.

By 70 B.C. Pompey and Crassus were Rome's two political poles (though Pompey was in Asia until 67, he was a power nonetheless), each with vast resources of money and troops at his disposal and each aiming at absolute political power. The two adversaries were so evenly matched that victory was uncertain, so they decided to cooperate—at least for the time being. Elected coconsuls for the year 70, they both viewed the Senate as a potential danger: neither would be able to control it, but either might use the Senate's power against the other. Crassus and Pompey coldbloodedly decided to hedge against the Senate's authority by taking control of the great unorganized energy of the Roman mob.

Crassus benefited greatly during this period from the help of one Gaius Julius Caesar, a young man from a noble family who was nevertheless extremely popular with the Roman populace.

The wars against Carthage had strained the economy, political structure, and military might of the Roman Republic. When the Gracchus brothers tried to remedy these problems with their reforms, they threatened the hold of the Senate on the Roman government. When the Senate struck down the Gracchi using illegal means, it in effect legitimized violence as part of the political process. The shift from mob violence to military force was institutionalized by the likes of Marius and Sulla, and an army became a tool to circumvent the legislative process—an instrument of dictatorship.

CHAPTER VI

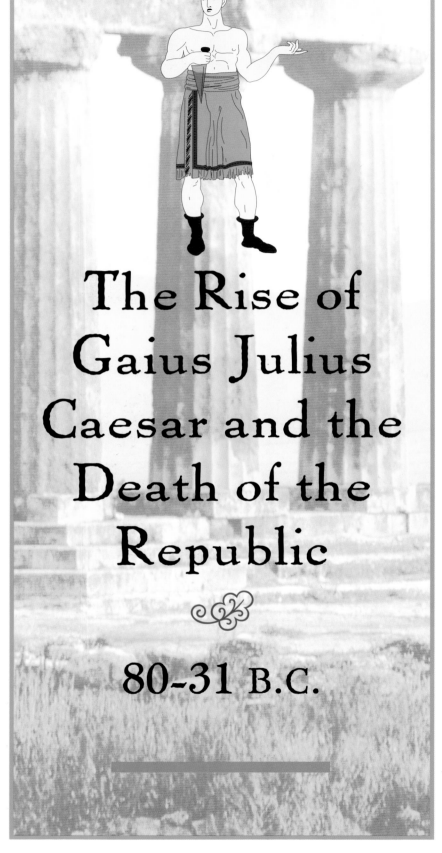

The Rise of
Gaius Julius
Caesar and the
Death of the
Republic

80-31 B.C.

BETWEEN 70 AND 31 B.C., certain factions in Rome tried to restore the republican senatorial form of government, with its elaborate system of checks and balances. Unfortunately, violence and greed had become so entrenched in Roman political life that the republican form of government could not be revived. Only one system of rule would survive in the vicious new world of Roman politics—a dictatorship expressing the will of a single ruler.

THE FIRST TRIUMVIRATE

Crassus and his young friend Caesar, aware that Pompey was a potential rival, awaited his return from Asia with apprehension. Outwardly, they manifested no sign of hostility, but secretly they schemed against him at every opportunity. At the same time, the Senate was strengthening its own hand, utilizing the considerable eloquence of Marcus Tullius Cicero (106–43 B.C.), who spoke for the old republican forms of government.

In 62 B.C., Pompey returned to Italy, disbanded his army according to tradition, and entered Rome as a private citizen hoping, with some justification, to be rewarded for his service in the east. He had every reason for optimism since his victories had more than doubled the revenue of the Roman state, not only from the spoils of the conquests themselves but also through the annual taxes that he had imposed upon the subject provinces. He was stunned when the Senate, fearful that he would use his army veterans to stage a coup, refused to grant him land with which to reward those soldiers for their hard years of service.

Faced with this senatorial opposition, Pompey decided to join forces with Crassus and Caesar against the Senate; the next two years saw a subtle tug of war between the Senate and these three men. In 60 B.C., they formed an informal alliance called the Triumvirate, from the Latin for "of three men." To this association, Caesar brought broad-based political alliances with the lower classes; Pompey, the immense popular appeal of a successful general; and Crassus, an immense fortune. The Triumvirate was a delicate balance of power that allowed them to oppose the Senate while checking the ambition of any one of the three.

Their natural allies in this struggle were the great urban masses living a hand-to-mouth existence in Rome. The three associates began to court the poor by pushing through laws favorable to them, such as the dole of free grain for every free Roman male and free public games and entertainment. This courtship was expensive, and the triumvirs realized that they would soon need more money—and where better to obtain it than through foreign conquests? In 56 B.C., by exerting political pressure, the Triumvirate received permission from the people's assemblies to wage foreign campaigns. Their avowed purpose was to strengthen the Republic

and defend it from enemies, but in reality their goal was to fill their personal coffers.

Caesar received Gaul as his arena; Pompey, that region of Spain that the Romans had not conquered; and Crassus, the eastern section of Syria, then held by the Parthians. Like the gangsters of the American Twenties, the three men split up the available "business," only instead of a single area of a single city, these players divided up substantial pieces of territory on three continents. Each went to his respective "corner" hoping to conquer a fortune. In 53 B.C., when Crassus was killed at the Battle of Carrhae in Mesopotamia, near modern Edessa, along with thirty thousand from his forty-thousand-man army, Pompey and Caesar were left on the field.

In Rome, their interests were watched over by two rival "gangs" that took turns fighting each other and intimidating the Senate. Rome was descending into chaos. In 53 and 52 B.C. the atmosphere was so hazardous that newly elected officials could not assume power. Finally, in January 52, Publius Clodius, a partisan of Caesar, was killed in a brawl with Titus Annius Milo, a supporter of Pompey. The city erupted into riots and the Senate house was burned to the ground. Realizing that they had to choose one side or the other, the Senators opted for Pompey, and order was temporarily restored.

THE RISE OF GAIUS JULIUS CAESAR

Meanwhile, Caesar was conquering Gaul in a series of brilliant campaigns against incredible odds, victories that demonstrated not only Caesar's military ability but also the discipline and courage of the Roman army. At one point in 52 B.C., while besieging the Gallic town of Alesia, the Roman army was itself surrounded by

another Gallic army; the Romans, fighting in two directions at once, won a resounding victory. Caesar was careful to keep the population of Rome apprised of his successes; his still famous *Commentarii de bello Gallico (The Commentaries on the Gallic Wars)* was written as a propaganda piece, sent to Rome, and copied onto the city walls so that everyone who could read was able to share in Caesar's triumphs.

In 49 B.C. Caesar, a military hero thanks to this propaganda, returned to Rome, where Pompey's henchmen had introduced resolutions into the Senate demanding that Caesar disband his army upon his return. For Caesar to have done so while Pompey still had an army to command, however, would have been foolhardy, since political murders were everyday occurrences. On January 1, 49 B.C., the Senate threatened to declare Caesar a public enemy if he did not disband his army. On January 10 Caesar, defying the Senate, crossed the Rubicon, the small river just below Ravenna on the east coast of Italy that marked the boundary between Cisalpine Gaul and Italy. Traditionally, Roman generals were not allowed to take troops across the Rubicon into Italy; Caesar's doing so was an act of defiance that initiated a civil war.

Caesar had only a single legion with him; Pompey had two. The bulk of Pompey's army was still in Spain, yet Caesar acted so quickly and decisively that Pompey lost heart, retreated south to Brundisium, and then moved across the Adriatic Sea to Greece. Four years of war followed, with Caesar chasing Pompey from one end of the Mediterranean to the other. By the end of 49 B.C., he had followed Pompey to Spain, beaten him at the Battle of Ilerda, and moved on to Greece, where he beat him again at Pharsalus in August 48. From there, Pompey fled to Egypt, where he hoped to find safety. The pharaoh Ptolemy XIII (r. 51–47 B.C.),

however, thinking to gain favor with Caesar, ordered Pompey killed and his head cut off to be preserved in brine—as a gift for Caesar. Caesar, who had no plans to kill Pompey, was horrified when he arrived in Egypt. He ordered the execution of the men who had carried out the murder and in time saw to the elimination of Ptolemy XIII.

With Pompey dead and Egypt under the control of the pro-Roman queen, Cleopatra, Caesar found himself in effect master of the entire Mediterranean Basin by the spring of 47 B.C. It was in Egypt that Caesar formed the famous amorous and political alliance with Cleopatra, whom he invited to return with him to Rome in 46, an act that angered the Roman people, who disapproved of her foreign appearance and mistrusted what they perceived as her corrupting eastern influence on a rough-and-ready Roman soldier. Caesar left Egypt and traveled back to Rome via Pontus, in Asia Minor, where he stopped briefly to conduct a five-day campaign against Pharnaces, a local despot and former ally of Pompey during the civil war who had raided Roman territory. At the conclusion of the Battle of Zela, he sent back to the Senate in Rome his famous report on the battle, "Veni, Vidi, Vici"—"I came, I saw, I conquered." Perhaps he meant it as a warning that he expected to deal just as easily with enemies in Rome.

The Rise of Gaius Julius Caesar and
the Death of the Republic

Arriving in Rome, he quickly forced the Senate to pass a number of reforms. Realizing that the unsettled times had driven many into debt, he canceled all rent for the poor for a year and deferred the interest on debts for the same length of time. In 46 and 45 B.C. he continued his programs of reform while increasing his own power. The Senate voted him the title dictator for ten years, appointed him prefect of morals for three, and gave him the right to speak first in their debates on any topic. He raised the number of senators from six hundred to nine hundred and allowed Italians and Gauls from northern Italy to become members. This action packed the Senate with men who were personally grateful to Caesar and could be counted on to support his programs.

Caesar saw to the welfare of his veteran soldiers by giving them land in Italy and in colonies overseas. Each of his veterans also received a bonus of five thousand denarii, an impressive sum at a time when a common soldier earned only 125 denarii a year. He also regulated the distribution of free grain, reformed the laws governing business and the collection of taxes, launched a huge new building program to give the poor work, and introduced a new calendar, named for him, of 365 days a year, with an extra day in February every four years. This is the Julian calendar that we still use today. It appeared that Rome had returned to the days of solid government presiding over a peaceful environment.

THE RISE OF OCTAVIUS

Unfortunately, the health of the Republic depended solely on the health of Julius Caesar. Although there were Romans who dreamed of a rebirth of senatorial power, that period was long past; after nearly a century of impotence and civil disorder, the Senate was inca-

pable of effective and decisive action. Consequently, when a small group of conspirators assassinated Caesar on March 15, 44 B.C., the Republic, its foundations eroded, quickly toppled and crumbled back into the chaos of civil war.

Initially, Marcus Tullius Cicero, lawyer, senator, and orator, in conjunction with two of Caesar's assassins, Marcus Junius Brutus and Gaius Cassius, tried to reestablish senatorial rule. But the Senate soon began to argue with Marcus Antonius—more familiarly known as Mark Antony—one of Caesar's ablest associates, over Antony's role in the new government and over the amount of money to be set aside for pensions and land for Caesar's veterans. Furthermore, a new rival for power, Gaius Octavius Thurinus, the nineteen-year-old grandson of Julius Caesar's sister, Julia, also made a bid for power. He was, in fact, Caesar's adopted son and thus his legal successor according to the dictator's will, and would control the dictator's vast personal fortune.

For a time, it seemed that the Senate might make common cause with Octavius against Antony. Yet they unwisely hesitated, finally repudiating Octavius and driving the young man into an alliance with Antony, and with Marcus Aemilius Lepidus, Caesar's trusted cavalry commander. Together, the three men formed the Second Triumvirate, a committee (so they said) to reconstruct the Republic. They backed their claim with their collective military strength of thirty-three legions.

Faced with this massed power, the senatorial leaders, Brutus and Cassius, withdrew from Rome to Greece to raise an army large enough to offer resistance. With the Senate leadership gone, the three triumvirs held complete sway in Rome. To the horror of all, they revived the process of proscription made infamous by Sulla forty years earlier, ordering the execution of 130 senators and two thousand equites. Publicly they announced that the deaths were punishments for the murder of Caesar, but the real reason for the executions was to raise money by the sale of the confiscated property of the condemned to finance a war against the senatorial party. One of the first candidates for execution was Cicero.

Meanwhile, Brutus and Cassius were looting Greece to raise money to equip their army of nineteen legions. In 42 B.C., Antony and Octavius crossed from Italy to Greece and defeated the senatorial army at Philippi, in north central Macedonia. Cassius and Brutus, knowing what awaited them, committed suicide. Having disposed of the senatorial threat, Octavius returned to Italy to raise more money, while Antony traveled to the Roman province of Asia to do the same. No doubt both men knew they would soon have to fight each other, but strangely, neither felt threatened by the third member of the triumvirate, Lepidus, who was singularly unambitious. Lepidus, sent to Africa to pacify the region, was content to live out his life there in obscurity — and safety.

Both Antony and Octavius, however, had plans. In Italy, Octavius faced Antony's brother, Lucius, and Sextus Pompeius Magnus, Pompey's son, who controlled a huge fleet and a series of campaigns in Illyricum, roughly western modern Yugoslavia. Antony, meanwhile, was in the eastern Mediterranean,

initiating actions against Parthia, conquering Armenia, and, in 41, falling under Cleopatra's spell. In her late twenties, the pharaoh was more attractive than ever and just as determined to get the best political deal for Egypt, although by all accounts she was genuinely devoted to Antony. Placing the considerable economic resources of Egypt at Antony's disposal, she became his lover, confidant, and political counselor.

Back in Italy, Octavius was consolidating his power. He had recently married, apparently for love, Livia Drusilla, a noblewoman with a huge fortune. The fact that when he met her she was married to one of his closest friends, Tiberius Claudius Nero (42 B.C.–A.D. 37), and pregnant with her husband's child, proved only a minor difficulty for Octavius. Tiberius and Livia were persuaded to divorce, Octavius adopted the child, and Livia became one of Octavius' closest advisors, assuming a more prominent role than any Roman woman before her. With Cilinus Maecenas, Marcus Vipsanius Agrippa, and her ex-husband, she was one of a small band of advisors who helped Octavius plan his successful seizure of power by eliminating Antony.

Antony was neither treacherous nor interested in Octavius' third of the Roman world — in fact, as a gesture of good faith he married Octavius' sister Octavia in 40 B.C. during his very public affair with Cleopatra. Octavius, however, was unwilling to share power with anyone, and he was especially reluctant to leave anyone in control of Egypt, with its vast agricultural and mineral wealth. Octavius set to work to discredit Antony in the eyes of the Roman people as a prelude to open war. Antony played into his hands. In 32, he renounced Octavia to marry Cleopatra, who was not only a foreigner, but one whom the Roman people hated already from her association with Julius Caesar and by whom he had fathered two children. In essence, the Romans no longer considered Antony a Roman, so dazzled was he by Egypt's queen and ways.

OCTAVIUS CLOSES IN FOR THE KILL

Octavius had all the ammunition he needed, as well as Rome's traditional contempt for women, for his propaganda campaign against Cleopatra, whom he portrayed as a depraved Eastern temptress who sought, perhaps through witchcraft, to seduce Antony and be queen of the world. The mood of the Roman populace swung dramatically against Antony, and perhaps overly confident of the affection his soldiers held for him, he did little to counter Octavius' slanders, even though he had numerous friends in high places in Rome.

In 32 B.C., Octavius appeared before the Senate to read Antony's will. Most historians believe the will that Octavius read was a forgery, but after Octavius' barrage of propaganda, the Roman people were only too willing to believe anything of Antony. In his will, Antony supposedly declared his children by Cleopatra to be his true heirs and Caesar's son by Cleopatra, Caesarion, to be Caesar's true heir and thus the inheritor of Caesar's vast fortune. The will further declared that Antony desired to be buried next to Cleopatra in the mausoleum of the Ptolemies. The enraged Romans, believing themselves betrayed, enthusistically supported Octavius' declaration of war against Antony.

Octavius and Antony sent their armies to Greece. Antony's forces outnumbered Octavius', but Octavius' troops were under the command of Marcus Agrippa, considered the best military leader of his time. Yet when the two forces met at Actium on the west coast of Greece in a titanic sea battle, it was not Agrippa's superior generalship that defeated Antony but a plague

among Antony's crews, dissension and jealousy among his admirals, and the unmaneuverabiltiy of Cleopatra's oversize Egyptian ships, compared with the smaller, agile Roman ones.

Antony fled to Egypt, and in the summer of 30 B.C., Octavius followed. Antony seemed unable to mount an effective defense, and his legions deserted to Octavius; abandoned and relentlessly pursued, Antony committed suicide. A few days later, Cleopatra, apparently mourning Antony and refusing to endure the shame of being displayed in Octavius' Roman triumph, likewise killed herself. Despite the legend that she ordered a poison asp to be smuggled to her in a basket of fruit, Cleopatra seems to have used a cobra instead. The poison of an asp produces a painful, slow death, usually preceded by loss of bowel control. The poison of the cobra is quick, painless, and neat—Cleopatra wanted to exit with dignity.

In 31 B.C., Octavius, like his great-uncle and adoptive father, Julius Caesar, thirteen years before, was the undisputed master of the Roman Republic. Yet unlike his famous uncle, Octavius would have not six months but the luxury of forty-five years to consolidate his victory. Octavius knew, as Caesar had, that the old republican government was hopelessly antiquated and unworkable. What it needed was a complete overhaul.

Above: By committing suicide, Cleopatra VII (69–30 B.C.) "cheated" Octavius out of his plan to parade her through the streets of Rome in a military triumph. He allowed her to be buried, along with Mark Antony, in traditional Egyptian style. The recent discovery in Alexandria's harbor of her tomb and palace will hopefully reveal more about her.

The Rise of Gaius Julius Caesar and the Death of the Republic

CHAPTER VII

Octavius Augustus and the Birth of the Roman Empire

31 B.C.–A.D. 14

Pages 106–107: The Ara Pacis, or Altar of Peace, was completed in 9 B.C. and commemorated Augustus' return from campaigns in Spain and Gaul. The reliefs on the altar illustrate the actual consecration procession.

UPON HIS RETURN TO Rome after defeating Antony and Cleopatra, Octavius set to redesigning the government. Although the old republican system of government was clearly obsolete, he shied away from radical change, preferring to preserve the outward form of government while revising its inner workings and power structure. His changes would prove to be highly efficient, successful foundations of a Roman government that would last for the next three hundred years.

OCTAVIUS' REFORM OF THE GOVERNMENT

Now that he had won the world, what was Octavius to do with it? He realized, with his usual political astuteness, that first and foremost Rome wanted peace and stability after more than a century of chaos or the threat of chaos since the aftermath of Tiberius Gracchus' reforms. Behind the outward appearances of the old Republic, he gathered all power into his own hands. The Senate, controlled by his partisans and fearful of another purge, supported him utterly. First, the senators named him *imperator*, or commander of all the armies, and second, they ceded him control of the *aerarium*, the state treasury. To the state monies he added the phenomenal sum of 1,400,000,000 sesterces that he had captured in Egypt, an amount of money so vast that when shipped to Rome it caused the interest rate to fall from 12 to 4 percent.

Octavius asked for and received the title of principes, or first citizen, a title that carried with it the authority, parallel to the Senate's, to initiate legislation that would be submitted to the various people's assemblies. Though he stipulated that the Senate could enact laws on its own without the approval of the people's assemblies, he encouraged that body to respect the traditional process. The title principes gave its name to his administration, known as the Principate. In addition to this honor, the Senate voted him *imperium maius*, which enabled him to act as proconsul throughout Rome's Empire. In the pre-Principate Republic, a proconsul was one who either functioned as consul in a specific province or, more usually, as commander of a specific army. With this title, however, Octavius outranked any general commanding any Roman army throughout the Empire.

Not to be outdone by the Senate in bestowing honors on Octavius, the Concilium Plebis Tributa voted him the *tribunicia potestas*, which enabled him to speak before and institute legislation in the people's assembly. The title meant he could veto the acts of any other government official, but it had far-reaching implications as well, for it made his body sacrosanct—any attempt on his life was thenceforth not only a terrible impiety but also a capital crime against the state.

Octavius stated that he intended to rule with the advice and consent of the Senate, and he always displayed the greatest respect for that body, even during his periodic purges of it. In 28 B.C., he dismissed two hundred senators who had been appointed by one or another of the triumvirs between 43 and 31 B.C. In 18 and 13 B.C., he further reduced the membership, and the number of senators fell to about six hundred. He passed laws that restricted membership in the Senate to men of good moral character who possessed fortunes of at least 800,000 sesterces, an amount later raised to 1,000,000.

He also saw to it that the Senate and various people's assemblies passed laws such as the *Lex Papia Poppaea*, which required bachelors to marry, prohibited long engagements, and ordered all widows and widowers to marry within three years of the spouse's death. Violators of these laws became ineligible to inherit money and property left to them in wills and were barred from the public games. To encourage childbearing among the noble classes and the equites, Octavius offered incentives based on the number of children a family had.

Octavius advocated moral behavior that he believed contributed to the stability of Rome, but he also stressed the idea of divine retribution for sin: the recent civil wars represented such a punishment. When his own daughter Julia was accused of immoral conduct, he banished her to a remote island in the Mediterranean for the rest of her life. To encourage morality and discourage crime, he organized the first formal police force in Rome.

THE MAKING OF AN EMPEROR

On January 13, 27 B.C., Octavius made a dramatic appearance before the Senate in which he surrendered all his powers to that body. The Senate accepted but—no doubt by prior agreement—"forced" him to accept proconsular power for ten years over Gaul, Spain, and Syria. These provinces held twenty of the twenty-six legions of the Roman army, so command of these troops ensured political control of the new Empire as well. Egypt, Rome's richest territory, remained Octavius' personal property and independent of the Senate's authority. Although the Senate assumed con-

trol of all the other provinces of the Empire and of Italy itself, these areas together held only six legions.

Three days after his dramatic gesture and the Senate's equally dramatic response, the senators voted Octavius one more honor—the right to use the title *Augustus*, meaning "consecrated" or "holy one," as part of his name. From that date, Octavius used the name Augustus, and by that name he is known as the first Roman emperor.

MILITARY AND FOREIGN AFFAIRS

With Rome's domestic affairs apparently settled, Augustus turned to foreign affairs. Happily, the only major power contiguous with Roman territory was the Parthian empire in Mesopotamia, whose ruler, Phraates IV (r. 398–2 B.C.), signed a peace treaty. Thus, Rome enjoyed peace on its eastern frontier for the next century.

The only other foreigners that concerned Rome for the next hundred years were the barbarians of central Europe and those along the African frontier. The desert tribes along the southern border of the Empire in North Africa were easily contained, while the coast of Mauretania, extending to the Atlantic Ocean, was held by a firm ally of Rome, Juba II (r. 25–23 B.C.), a member of the Mauretanian royal family who was also a Roman citizen. Juba married Cleopatra Selene (the daughter of Cleopatra and Antony), and their son, Ptolemy, would rule Mauretania in Rome's interests until A.D. 40.

Below: Head of the young Octavius, about age seventeen. Octavius was the grandnephew of Julius Caesar, and, on Caesar's death, was the dictator's closest living male relative. Julius Caesar, lacking legitimate heirs, formally adopted Octavius on September 13, 45 B.C. This adoption was one reason why Caesar's troops supported the nineteen-year-old's bid for power when Caesar died.

Unfortunately, Varus' unreasonable demands on the conquered Germans excited them to rebellion; under the leadership of Arminius, they massacred three legions at the Battle of the Teutoburg Forest. The Roman border quickly contracted to the Rhine, where it would remain until the fall of the Empire.

Augustus was well aware that the army that had allowed him to seize power could serve the same function for someone else. Early in his reign he had taken the precaution of stationing twenty of the army's twenty-six legions in provinces he personally controlled. Next, he set up two special treasuries, also under his personal control, to pay the legions and provide pensions, land, or both to soldiers who had completed their twenty-five-year hitch in the army.

CHANGING THE FACE OF ROME

Once in firm control of the government, Augustus was determined to advertise and justify his power by beautifying Rome. From the time of the Gracchus brothers to Augustus' triumphant conclusion of the civil wars, there had been little construction in Rome — the money was needed for other things during those chaotic times. Augustus certainly had wealth; both Egypt's vast resources and the annual receipts of the treasury were his to use as he chose. He launched an impressive building campaign that, when completed, allowed him to boast, "I found Rome a city of brick and left it one of marble."

His most impressive building projects were the Forum Augusti, or Forum of Augustus; the Temple of Apollo; the Temple of Mars; and the Templum Divi Iulii, or Temple of the Divine Julius. A fixture of Roman cities and towns, forums were open places where business and government were conducted.

On the southern border of Egypt, Gaius Petronius, the governor of Egypt, successfully repulsed the Ethiopian army of Queen Candace; captured her capital, Napata, in 22 B.C.; and firmly established the First Cataract of the Nile as the border between the two countries.

That left the Germanic tribes in central Europe, whose constant raids caused Augustus to extend the borders of the Empire to the Rhine and the Danube, reinforcing those natural lines of defense with garrisons and with a fleet on each river. In A.D. 9, Augustus sent Publius Quintilius Varus across the Rhine to the Elbe because this river seemed more defensible.

The Forum Augusti was surrounded by beautiful temples and public buildings; at the eastern end stood the great temple to Mars, *Mars Ultor*, housing giant statues of Mars and Venus, the legendary parents of the Roman people, as well as a statue of their most famous offspring, Julius Caesar. The temple was basically Greek in appearance, but had a semicircular apse at one end, an innovation at the time and one that became progressively more popular, eventually inspiring church architecture.

Perhaps the most famous architectural structure that Augustus built was the Ara Pacis Augustae, or Altar of the Augustan Peace, which stood in the Campus Martius, or Field of Mars, at the beginning of the Via Flaminia. Walls of white Carrara marble, covered with reliefs of Augustus' extended family and members of the Senate, surrounded this sacred precinct. One of the reliefs depicts dedication of the altar, which took place on July 4, 13 B.C.. The lifelike sculpture captures every possible human expression—from the boredom of the children to their mothers' anxiety to the dignity of the senators.

Augustus, too frugal to spend only his own money on beautifying the city, encouraged his friends and supporters to do the same. One of the most impressive structures of this period—or any other—was the Pantheon, which Marcus Agrippa, Augustus' closest friend, built in 27 B.C. Only the front portico remains of the building Agrippa financed, for the temple burned in A.D. 80, but Pliny the Elder has left a description. The temple had bronze capitals on the columns, caryatids on the roof, and a magnificent mosaic floor. It was a political structure as well: built to honor all the gods of Rome, its interior was filled with statues of the major deities from throughout the Empire.

One of the most popular achievements of Augustus' building program was the Thermae Agrippae, the baths built by and named for Marcus Agrippa. They were the first major public baths in Rome, and the custom caught on; frequenting the public baths became the major social activity of lower-class Romans. Tiberius, Augustus' successor, found that building baths was a fine way to gain the support of the people, and their architecture became increasingly elaborate as time went on. Eventually, they became huge complexes, with marble floors, mosaics, and statues of gods, as well as the equivalent of today's malls, filled with food and novelty shops. Any Roman could spend an entire day at the baths for only a quadrans.

THE AGE OF AUGUSTAN LITERATURE

Augustus sponsored Roman literature as well. He enjoyed it, having received a fine classical education in Greece before entering politics. He therefore encouraged writers of all genres. Two of the greatest poets of all time, Quintus Horatius Flaccus (65–8 B.C.) and Publius Vergilius Maro (70–19 B.C.), flourished during his reign.

Publius Vergilius Maro, better known simply as Virgil, began his literary career in 38 B.C. with the publication of his *Bucolica (Pastoral Scenes)*, which celebrated life in the country and compared its simple pleasures to city life in Rome. When his little book of poems met with some success, his friends encouraged him to write more and introduced him to the right people in Rome. Shy and suffering from an embarrassing stammer, Virgil was not a social success. He was awkward around women and so unsuccessful in love that his friends nicknamed him "the virgin," perhaps in part a play on his name. Virgil left Rome for a time and adventures of Aeneas, the heroic prince of Troy, who survived the Greek sack of that city to wander across the Mediterranean in search of a new home for himself and his followers. The new home, of course, was Rome, and the admirable qualities of Aeneas and his followers mirror the qualities that allowed Rome to rule the Mediterranean during Augustus' era.

At the opposite end of the poetic spectrum was the urbane Quintus Horatius Flaccus, or Horace, who captured the attention of Maecenas, one of Augustus' closest advisors and confidantes. Fascinated by Horace's *Satires* of 30 B.C., Maecenas encouraged him to write more and even arranged for the poet to live on a small estate near the Tiber, east of Rome. While living there, he composed a second book of satires and another collection of poems, the *Odes*. While the *Odes* have many subjects, a good number of them celebrate Augustus and his victories.

composed his celebrated *Georgics (The Farming Life)*, which idealized the rustic life in enduring lines such as:

> *Happiest is the fellow who knows*
> *The country life and counts the*
> *Temptations of this hellish world as*
> *Fit only for his feet to stamp on*

When Virgil's poetry gained Augustus' attention, Virgil's friends arranged a meeting between the shy poet and the world conqueror. Augustus, transfixed by the poet's reading, ordered him to compose an epic poem in praise of the spirit, fortitude, and power of the Romans. The result was the famous *Aeneid*, eleven years in the composing, in which Virgil, emulating Homer's *Iliad*, praises Roman virtue through the

Augustus also encouraged prose writers, and his era saw a number of them, not the least of whom was the emperor himself. The finest prose writer of this period was Livy, whose work traced the history of Rome from its earliest days to his own time. *De Urbe Condita (From the Foundation of the City)* presents dramatic, glowing accounts of the kings and heroes of the early Roman Republic. Livy and the emperor were both concerned with the decline in morality, and Livy sought to inspire his contemporaries to emulate the behavior of the ancient Romans. His work was so popular that it

Octavius Augustus and the Birth of
the Roman Empire

enjoyed the ancient equivalent of paperback editions—small scrolls that were easily held in the hand.

Augustus' own *Res Gestae (Deeds)*—a well-crafted account of his rise to power, his political maneuverings once in power, and his defeats of Rome's enemies—was discovered among his papers after he died in A.D. 14.

AFTER AUGUSTUS

Augustus' legacy was a world that stood on a firm political, economic, and military footing. A stable government was in place that was generally supported by the Roman people, who remembered all too well, and with horror, the excesses of the civil wars. Of those who realized that Rome was no longer a Republic but a dictatorship disguised as one, few perhaps regretted the demise of a political system that in the end had bred disorder and death. Those who did mourn the Republic had long since learned by example to keep their thoughts to themselves.

The army controlled the borders of the Empire, assured the Roman peace, and stayed out of politics. The Roman economy was booming as commerce benefited from the political and social stability, the gifts of an administration that patrolled the trade routes on land and policed sea routes across the Mediterranean and into the Black Sea. Business profited from a stable currency that made the Roman denarius the preferred coin for commerce from beyond the Pillars of Hercules at the western end of the Mediterranean to the coast of Indochina. One problem remained: who would pick up the reins?

Ovid: A Banished Poet

Not all the poets who flourished during the reign of Augustus received his support. Ovid—Publius Ovidius Naso (43 B.C.– A.D. 17)—one of Rome's most popular poets, wrote *Metamorphoses*, an elegant series of tales of mythological transformations that tell us much about the Roman and Greek legends. But Ovid is best known for his poems about seduction and infidelity—written at precisely the same time as Augustus' campaign to encourage sexual morality. For example, Ovid's homage to his mistress, Corinna, *Amores (Loves)*, published in 14 B.C., which ridicules marital fidelity and celebrates promiscuity, was an instant success.

In 2 B.C., he published *Ars Amatoria (The Art of Love)*, his textbook on seduction, in which Ovid tells his male readers what type of conversation most pleases a woman, where to pick them up (to use the modern expression), how to groom and dress oneself ("Dress simply, but eloquently, bathe often, avoid makeup, brush your teeth, get a tan, wear expensive shoes, trim your beard, and file your nails"), how to listen, when to be sincere, and how to act the "day after." It was unfortunate for Ovid that Augustus' libertine daughter, Julia, and her daughter, also named Julia, both read the book and apparently raved about it. This brought the poet to Augustus' notice just when the emperor was preaching the sanctity of the Roman family. In A.D. 8, Augustus heard a rumor that Ovid had been sexually involved with Augustus' granddaughter Julia, whereupon Augustus exiled the poet to Tomi, a remote Roman outpost on the Black Sea. Ovid died there pining for Rome.

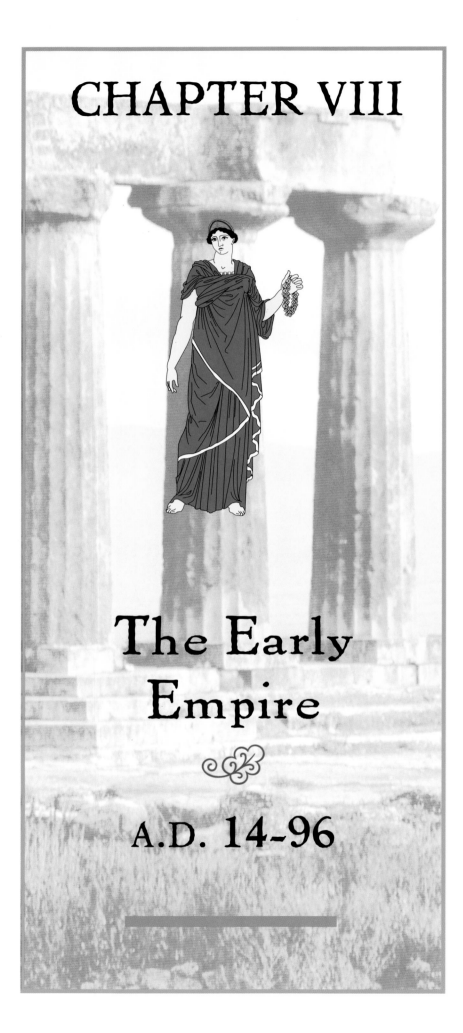

CHAPTER VIII

The Early Empire

A.D. 14-96

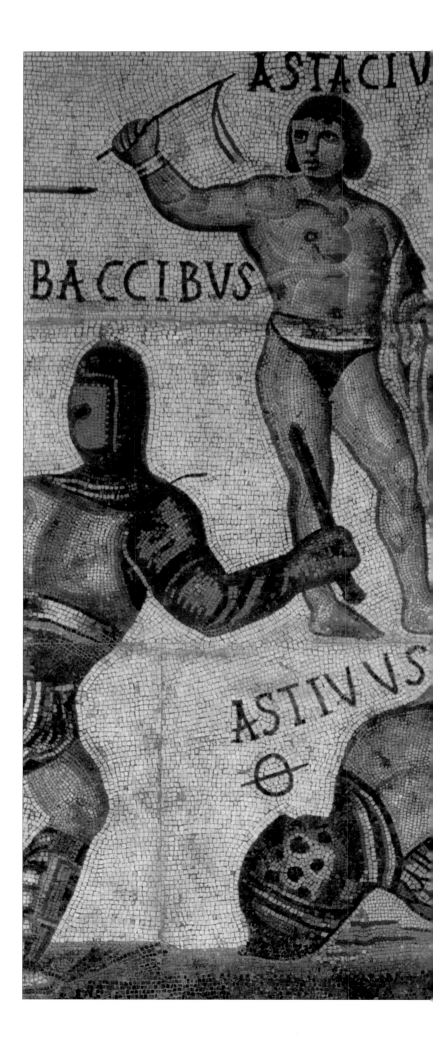

ASTACIV

BACCIBVS

ASTIVVS

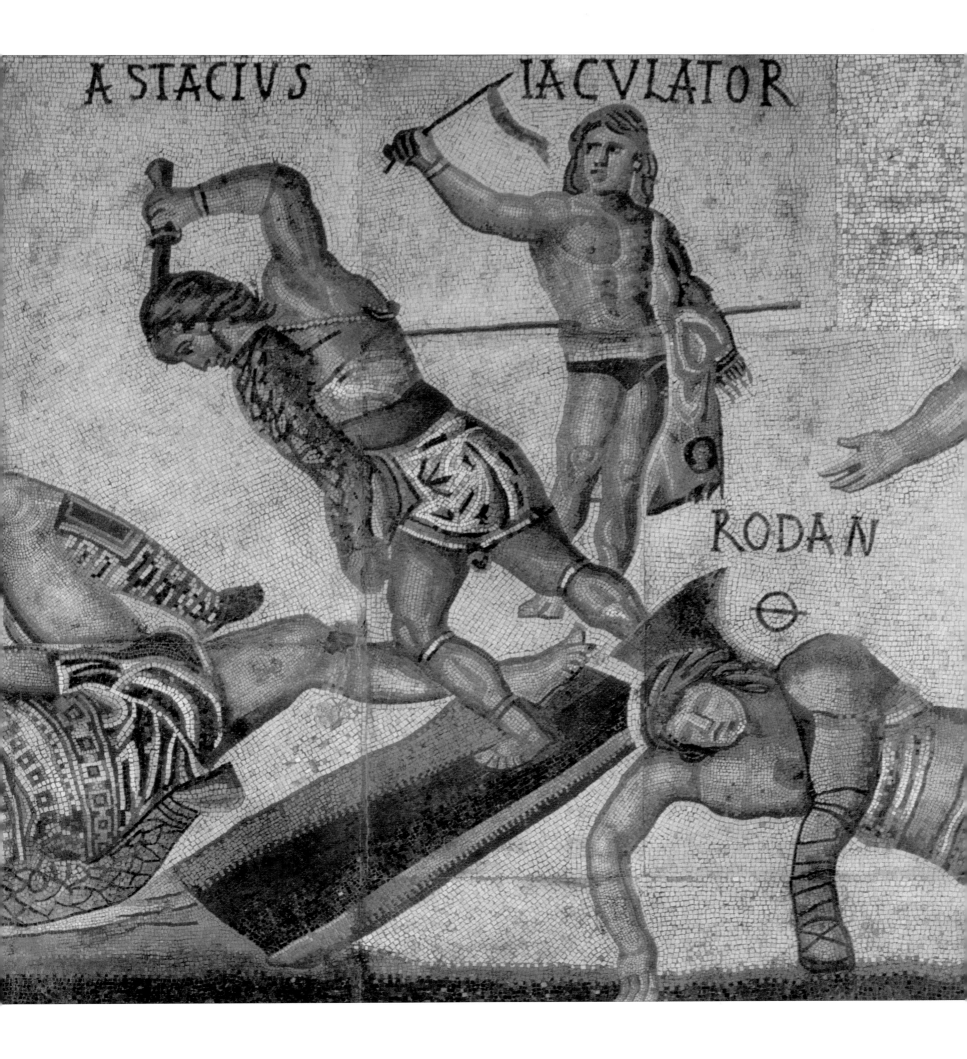

THE 150 YEARS FOLLOWING the death of Augustus revealed both the strengths and weaknesses of the system he had created. Hardworking and conscientious, he achieved wonders in the areas of administration, law, art, defense, and architecture. The economy flourished, the people prospered, and the borders of the Empire remained safe. That same centralized power in the hands of a succession of weak or even outright insane rulers, however, jeopardized the welfare of the Roman people and the security of the Empire. When, in the late third century A.D., the imperial frontiers began to give way to the pressure of invaders, the whole structure of the Roman world was threatened.

For more than fifty years after the death of Augustus, the Empire was ruled by relatives of both Augustus and Julius Caesar. Even when the genealogical connections were not close, they were reassuring to many and effective in determining succession among rival pretenders. For some years, blood relationship to the Caesars provided the political stability that many Romans longed for after the tumultuous time of Sulla and Marius and the ravages of the civil wars.

TIBERIUS CLAUDIUS NERO

The question of succession, and with it the potential for civil strife, immediately became an issue upon the death of Augustus. Although Augustus had named as his successor his stepson—Tiberius Claudius Nero, the son of Livia Drusilla by her first husband—Tiberius, taking no chances, ordered the deaths of Agrippa Postumus, the son of Augustus' faithful lieutenant, and of Julia, Augustus' daughter. The murders sparked several minor and easily contained rebellions in Rome and Pannonia (parts of modern Hungary and Yugoslavia) and along the Rhine River.

Obviously, some Romans still believed that family succession was incompatible with Roman tradition.

Once in office, Tiberius initially proved to be an excellent administrator. He limited government expenses by restricting the activities of the army and establishing easily defended borders. In addition, he streamlined government bureaucracy, severely punished dishonest Roman officials, and reduced government spending on public building programs and gladiatorial combats. At the same time, he increased the efficiency of food distribution in Rome and built roads and bridges throughout the Empire, which not only allowed troops to travel quickly through the Empire but also encouraged trade and commerce. He even instituted disaster relief for cities throughout the Empire that suffered from fire, famine, or earthquake.

Gradually, however, and mysteriously, Tiberius became increasingly autocratic and brutal. When, in A.D. 31, his trusted aide, Lucius Aelius Sejanus, attempted to initiate a coup to take the throne, Tiberius responded with a vicious purge of the government. He started with the execution of Sejanus and went on to order the execution of Sejanus' eleven-year-old son and seven-year-old daughter. Just as the executioner was about to strangle the little girl, someone in the crowd pointed out that Roman law forbade the execution of a virgin, whereupon the executioner raped the child and then strangled her.

Sejanus' betrayal seems to have triggered a paranoia in Tiberius that was to characterize the rest of his reign. To protect himself from assassination, Tiberius left Rome, eventually moving to his closely guarded estate on the island of Capri. He ordered the execution of all possible claimants to the throne, including two grandnephews; he spared the third, Gaius, considering him too young to be a threat, though he did keep the child under careful watch on Capri.

CALIGULA

Tiberius' successor was this very grandnephew, Gaius Caesar Augustus Germanicus, better known to history as Caligula, or "Little Boots"—a name given to him as a young boy by his father's soldiers because he wore tiny copies of soldier's boots around camp. This boy, whom Tiberius did not consider a threat, grew up to murder his uncle in 37. He poisoned the old emperor, then nearly eighty, at dinner and, when the poison did not act quickly enough, smothered him with a pillow. This violent act launched one of the most depraved reigns in Roman history.

In the end, Caligula's sadistic cruelty, vicious sense of humor, and arbitrary execution of members of the nobility brought him down. He apparently joked about supposed subversive plots of his senior officers to the point where these officers feared he might believe his own jests. These men, led by Cassius

The Early Empire

Chaerea—whom Caligula had repeatedly insulted by forcing him to kiss the imperial middle finger, held out in imitation of a penis—fell upon him with daggers on January 24, 41, as he left the gladiatorial games. His personal guards deserted him and began looting the palace; in the process, one of them drew aside a curtain, and found Tiberius Claudius Drusus Nero Germanicus, the emperor's uncle, shaking with fear behind it. The soldier led him back to the camp, where an assembly of troops proclaimed him emperor after he promised each soldier 150 aurei, the equivalent of twenty-five years' pay. Under these inauspicious circumstances, the emperor Claudius began an exceptionally successful reign.

CLAUDIUS

Claudius (10 B.C.– A.D. 54) survived the murderous reign of Caligula by pretending to be half-witted so that Caligula never saw him as a threat. Claudius' physical appearance helped in this deception: having suffered from polio as a child, one of his legs was shorter than the other, which caused him to stumble frequently. He was also unable to close his mouth completely and constantly drooled as a result. In addition he had a perpetual runny nose, a nervous tic that affected his head, and a speech defect that made him sound like an idiot; he also stammered.

What Caligula missed was that Claudius' disabled exterior concealed a brilliant mind. Claudius had

The Crimes of Caligula

Gaius Suetonius Tranquillus (c. A.D. 69–after 122), the author of *De vitae Caesarum* (*The Lives of the Caesars*), recounted a gruesome list of Caligula's crimes. For his own amusement, he built a bridge over an arm of the sea at Puteoli (modern Pozzuoli), invited the locals to cross it, and while they were doing so commanded his soldiers to throw them into the water. When they tried to climb out, the soldiers pushed them back in to drown. On a whim, he once ordered a hill leveled and then rebuilt nearby. He abused the Roman nobility by first seducing their wives, then criticizing the women's sexual performance in public.

He forced Roman senators to fight in the arena as gladiators or run for miles behind his chariot in their heavy woolen togas. He enjoyed having prisoners tortured before him at dinner, kept a master headsman constantly in attendance to decapitate people, and once, during a banquet, ordered a

slave's hands cut off on suspicion that the man had stolen a piece of silver off a table. He then had the slave led around the banquet tables with his severed hands hung around his neck, with a sign explaining the mutilation. Suetonius' list goes on: Caligula stole wives from their husbands and turned the imperial palace into a whorehouse, forcing the most virtuous aristocratic ladies of Rome to submit to "clients."

He seduced all three of his sisters, but was not fond of his sisters Agrippina and Livilla, so he lent them to his friends. On the other hand, Caligula loved Drusilla very much: when she died, he made it a capital crime during the official period of mourning to laugh or eat dinner with one's family. Later, he declared her a goddess. He believed himself to be the sun god and forbade people to look directly into his face, lest they be blinded. Strangest of all, he made it a capital crime to tell jokes about goats.

Right: Valeria Messalina was the third wife of the emperor Claudius and the mother of his only son, Britannicus (A.D. 41–55). Roman tradition presents her as a sadistic voluptuary, but this may be the result of imperial propaganda after her death in A.D. 48 at the hands of Claudius' subordinates, who resented her influence over her husband. Nero then poisoned Britannicus because he feared the boy's claim to the throne.

spent the reigns of Tiberius and Caligula absorbed in the study of history and shrewdly observing his fellow nobles; he realized that Rome had become powerful by adapting her government and economy to new situations. As emperor, he immediately set about instituting changes that streamlined the Roman government, making it more responsive to the needs of the Empire.

Aware that the Senate was dominated by selfish aristocrats who made decisions based on greed, Claudius purged that body and filled it with new senators. Many of these were wealthy Gauls from northern Italy who, with their elevated status, now felt an allegiance not only to Claudius but to the Roman state in whose government they now shared. Claudius also decreased the Senate's influence on the state by reorganizing the treasury, or *aerarium Saturni*, so that it was no longer run by senatorial appointees but by two quaestors appointed by himself to three-year salaried terms. In this way, he could allocate the nation's funds without hindrance or explanation.

And allocate them he did. During his reign he completed two aqueducts that Caligula had begun; built roads connecting Italy with Portugal, Spain, and the English Channel; and dug a canal joining the Meuse to the Rhine so that the agricultural center of Gaul could easily transport its products to the North Sea. His most famous project was transforming Ostia into an effective port to serve Rome. His engineers dredged

The Early Empire

the harbor, built concrete breakwaters, and constructed a series of warehouses to accommodate the grain the ships brought to feed Rome's hungry population.

Claudius continued his predecessors' policy of bread and games for the populace by expanding and beautifying the Circus Maximus, where the great chariot races were held. His engineers drained the Fucine Lake, north of Rome, turning 140,000 acres (56,000ha) of malarial swamp into farmland.

Claudius also made the government more efficient by staffing the bureaucracy with freedmen, ex-slaves who owed their freedom and success to Claudius personally. He hoped this would assure honesty through the personal loyalty that these men felt to him; although these people indeed proved efficient, the senators and equites who had previously run the government bitterly resented them.

Besides curtailing the power of a corrupt Senate and streamlining Roman government, Claudius stabilized the borders of the Empire and improved foreign relations between Rome and her only civilized neighbor, Parthia, which encompassed much of the area of modern Iraq, Iran, and eastern Turkey. To safeguard Rome's grain supply, Claudius expanded the Empire by annexing Thrace and the western and northern coasts of the Black Sea. With these areas added to Rome's existing possessions on the north coast of Turkey, the Black Sea became a Roman lake.

His military victory in Mauretania extended Roman rule to the Atlantic coast of North Africa.

THE CONQUEST OF BRITAIN

Perhaps Claudius' most famous conquest, however, was that of Britain, the only one to be motivated not by economic or political goals but by Claudius' desire for individual glory. To an ancient Roman, Britain was on the very edge of the known world. The fact that the armies of Claudius might conquer so distant and mysterious a place was a matter of immense pride, very similar to the pride the United States experienced when her astronauts landed on the moon in 1969. Julius Caesar's reputation was likewise enhanced when he led a raiding party to the island in 55 B.C.

In A.D. 43, Aulus Plautius took an army across the Channel and defeated a number of British tribes, taking advantage of the Celts' decentralized military habits, such as leaving key points unguarded and not presenting a united front. Plautius quickly advanced to the Thames River; sensing victory, he sent an urgent message to Claudius to hurry to Britain to lead the Roman army to victory. Claudius arrived, fought a sham duel against a badly wounded British chieftain, proclaimed victory, and returned triumphantly to Rome amid the delirious cheers of his subjects. It was political theater, and the mob loved it.

Below: A late Flavian Era (A.D. 69–96) sculpture of a Roman noblewoman sports an elaborate hairstyle. Wealthy women who owned many slaves could keep up with the latest fashions, which changed so quickly that some sculptors produced heads with detachable scalps in order to keep portraits up to date.

The Early Empire

UNLUCKY AT LOVE

Unfortunately, Claudius' personal life and his efforts to ensure a peaceful and orderly succession were less fortunate than his administrative and military exploits. Each of his four marriages was more scandalous than the last. He divorced his first two wives for their sexual escapades, but the behavior of his third wife, Valeria Messalina, was even more outrageous. Not only did she carry on numerous affairs with Roman nobles and equites, but she also enjoyed masquerading as a streetwalker under the aqueduct arches, or *fornices* (from which we get the word "fornicate"), where she sold herself to men of the lowest class.

Finally, she entered into a bigamous marriage with Gaius Silius, a Roman noble. Whatever her motive for this mad act, it prompted Claudius to order her murder; almost immediately he married his own niece, Agrippina the Younger. This lady proved his undoing, for in A.D. 54 she poisoned Claudius and arranged for the Senate and army to place her son by a previous marriage, Gnaeus Domitius Ahenobarbus, on the throne. When Claudius, at her urging, adopted the young man in A.D. 50, he was renamed Nero Claudius Drusus Germanicus Caesar, whom all ages know simply as Nero.

NERO

It was a testimony to the strength of the government Claudius had created that it continued to run efficiently during the fourteen long years that Nero (A.D. 37–68) was emperor. He was unquestionably insane for most of a reign marked by the effects of his sadism, megalomania, cowardice, paranoia, and sexual depravity. In the first five years of his reign, however, he was restrained by the influence of his mother and her supporters—the philosopher Lucius Annaeus Seneca, who served as Nero's tutor, and Sextus Afranius Burrus, prefect of the Praetorian Guard, the military unit responsible for Rome's internal security. Burrus, Seneca, and Agrippina made decisions that preserved the stability of the state; to

The Crimes of Nero

For the last ten years of his life, Nero engaged in every possible crime, including matricide disguised as a fatal accident. In 58, ostensibly for her enjoyment at her estate on the Bay of Naples, Nero gave Agrippina a yacht—constructed, however, that when one plank in the stern was removed, the entire vessel came apart. He hoped his mother would drown in a boating "accident," but to improve the odds, he had a large bar of lead secreted in the awning over the couch where Agrippina was likely to recline. The bar could be released by a long cord to fall on her head. Unfortunately for Nero, the plot went awry.

Late at night, as the boat cruised on the Bay of Naples, the captain released the bar, which missed Agrippina and hit her servant, Acerronia, instead. Dazed, Acerronia rushed around the deck screaming Agrippina's name; in the moonless dark, the crew mistook Acerronia for Agrippina and beat the poor girl to death with oars. The captain then pulled out the stern plank, and the boat began to collapse. As the vessel came apart, Agrippina took advantage of the darkness, slipped overboard, and swam to shore; the next morning, when Nero heard that his mother had escaped, he ordered troops to the house to kill her. They broke into the house and surrounded her bed, where, in her final dramatic and bitter moments, Agrippina asked the officer in charge to stab her in the womb whence the monster had come.

This grotesque and badly botched murder unhinged Nero, who descended into an orgy of murder and sexual depravity. When his pregnant wife, Poppaea, nagged him for returning home late from the races, he kicked her to death. He had Poppaea's son by a previous marriage drowned after spies reported that the boy had been play-acting as emperor. Nero also murdered his aunt, who suffered from chronic constipation, by ordering her doctors to give her a fatal dose of strong laxatives. He proposed marriage to Claudius' daughter, Antonia, and when she refused he had her executed for treason. He raped Aulus Plautius, one of his mother's lovers, and then had him killed. He ordered Seneca, his boyhood tutor, to commit suicide.

Nero reveled in sadistic displays, such as hiring an Egyptian ghoul who ate human flesh, and had still-living victims torn apart, forcing them to watch the monster eat their flesh. He illuminated his garden parties with human torches—living persons covered in pitch, hung from crosses, and ignited.

Nero was the emperor of Rome 54–68 A.D. He brought about the deaths of serveral prominent Romans, persecuted Christians, emptied the public treasury, and was implicated in the burning of Rome. He was finally declared a public enemy and committed suicide.

distract Nero from interfering they encouraged his fantasies of becoming a great musician, poet, and all-around man of letters.

The Great Fire

Ancient authors from Suetonius to Gaius Plinius Caecilius (A.D. 23–79) and Cassius Dio Cocceianus (A.D. 150–235) agreed that Nero's greatest crime was ordering the setting of the Great Fire that destroyed half of Rome between July 19 and 28, 64, and that this mad incendiary plot was part of the emperor's massive urban renewal project. He subsequently constructed, on a massive scale, a beautiful new city with dozens of fountains and squares, and required all houses to be rebuilt with stone first-story facades and wide streets and alleys between each block to prevent fire from spreading easily.

Nero also utilized the space created by the fire to build his famous *Domus aurea*, or "golden house," by far the most splendid palace ever built in Europe—not excluding Louis XIV's palace at Versailles. The house was surrounded by 120 acres (48ha) of lawns, parks, lakes, arcades, and hunting fields, all for the pleasure of one deranged ego. The entrance to this great dwelling was adorned by a 120-foot (36.5m) statue of Nero himself, a sculpture so impressive that seven years later, when the emperor Vespasian tore down the Domus aurea to build his great amphitheater, he kept the statue, thriftily cutting off Nero's head and replacing it with the head of Apollo.

The act forever associated in the popular mind with Nero—his persecution of the Christians in retaliation for setting the Great Fire—is generally unsupported by pagan sources. Only one Roman writer, the historian Cornelius Tacitus, relates the fire to the Christians at all, and the wording of his accusation has caused many Latinists to question his meaning.

Christianity only became a concern of the Roman state fifty years later, and then not because of fears of incendiary vandalism but because the secrecy in which early Christians practiced their religion and their refusal to worship the emperors made them suspect in a political environment seething with plots and counterplots against the government. All exclusive societies were suspect, and the Romans persecuted any group that met in secret. For instance, in 112 the emperor Trajan refused the request of a group of citizens in Antioch to form a fire department because he feared that the group could talk treason and sedition during their meetings.

Only four years after the Great Fire, in 69, Nero was dead, killed at his own request by his freedman Epaphroditus. When he died, Nero was facing widespread revolt in the Senate, whose members had grown anxious that the mad emperor might condemn them for some imagined treason. The armies also had grievances with Nero, who had neither paid them since 67 nor visited them on the frontiers, something that even the crippled Claudius had managed to do. Historians call the year 69 the Year of the Four Emperors, since in quick succession four different men in different parts of the Empire, each a commander supported by his legions, tried for the supreme position. When the dust settled in December 69, Rome had a new emperor and a new political power, as the army's approval became the greatest factor in the selection and retention of a Roman emperor.

VESPASIAN

The new emperor was Titus Flavius Sabinus Vespasianus (A.D. 9–79, r. 69–79), who was succeeded by his two sons. The founder of the Flavian dynasty was a professional soldier who had spent his life in the ranks, served in the army that conquered Britain, and later held command in Greece, Germany, Spain, Thrace, Africa, and the Middle East. Most recently he had served in Judea, where he fought the Jewish sect that called themselves the Zealots. At the first sign of rebellion against Nero, Vespasian, none of whose ancestors had been senators, had quickly thrown his hat in the ring and hurried to Egypt to seize control of that country's grain exports. From Egypt he moved his armies to Italy, there defeating the other would-be emperors.

After Nero's excesses, Rome needed a calm, decisive, and dependable man such as Vespasian at the helm. He had the support of the legions and was a hardworking administrator who viewed the emperorship as a job to be done well, not as an excuse for personal license. He also brought to the task a head for figures, and through fiscal reorganization and spending restraints he restored financial stability to an empire

Above: Titus Flavius Vespasianus (r. A.D. 69–79) made reform a major part of his reign, and after the excesses of Nero his rule was welcomed by upper-class Romans. He reintroduced discipline into an army that had grown lax under his predecessor, and he reformed the Empire's finances after Nero's profligate spending.

The Early Empire

nearly bankrupted by Nero. In particular, Vespasian was a genius at creating and collecting taxes (his father and grandfather were tax collectors): he is most famous for his tax on the public men's toilets he built. According to Suetonius, when Vespasian's son Titus objected to the imperial government stooping to collect money from such an undignified source, Vespasian took one of the coins so collected, held it under his son's nose, and asked, "Can you smell the piss?"

Vespasian saw the legions as a threat to the stability of the Empire. In the recent struggle for power, rival claimants had used the legions they commanded to further their claims to the throne. These men had often inspired their troops, recruited from the same provinces in which they served, by promising that if they succeeded, the government would address their specific local concerns. Vespasian inaugurated a policy of transferring officers and legions from the areas where they had been recruited to areas of the Empire far from their homelands. These reforms, with a few exceptions, would end the menace of provincial revolts on the part of "home-grown" legions for more than a century.

Vespasian also tied the provinces closer to Rome by granting citizenship to promising provincials and bringing them to serve in administrative posts in Rome. In this way, he hoped especially to turn Celts from Gaul and Germans from the Rhine into whole-hearted Romans. In addition, he invited the wealthiest of these provincials into the Senate, where he knew they would support his policies.

These military and administrative changes went a long way toward integrating the diverse parts of the Empire into a tight, nationalistic union whose borders Vespasian made increasingly secure. To protect the southern portion of Britain, his generals subdued the most populous areas of the island until only the sparsely settled areas north of an east–west line between the modern cities of Carlisle and Tynemouth were outside Roman control. In Syria and Mesopotamia, he established a more easily defensible frontier between the Roman and Parthian Empires.

At home in Rome, Vespasian, in the tradition of his predecessors, beautified the city, aware that this was what its inhabitants now expected of an emperor. He spent lavishly on temples and public buildings. Besides the Temple of Peace near the Roman Forum and a Temple of the Deified Claudius on the Caelian, Vespasian began construction on the famous Flavian Amphitheater—more commonly called the Colosseum. The facade was decorated with arcades flanked by three-quarter columns that are in the Doric style on the first level, in the Ionic on the second, and in the Corinthian on the third. On the topmost level there were wooden overhangs that protected spectators from the sun. From these wooden structures an awning could be stretched over the whole amphitheater to provide shade for both contestants and spectators.

Imperial Entertainments

The purpose of the Colosseum was to satisfy the blood lust of the Romans for fights to the death between gladiators or between *bestiarii* (animal fighters) and wild animals. Fifty thousand spectators could watch daylong shows in which well-trained, well-fed warriors engaged in duels, employing a variety of weapons and armor. These battles were usually to the death, unless both gladiators fought extraordinarily well or the defeated gladiator performed with exceptional skill. A victor himself might grant the defeated opponent

The Early Empire

Above: A Roman relief in the Museo Nazionale Romano delle treme shows *samnis*, or swordsmen, fighting. **Opposite:** Venus and Mars share an intimate moment in a wall painting from a villa at Pompeii. Venus and Mars are the legendary parents of Romulus and Remus, the legendary founders of Rome.

his life, or the crowd could demand it with cries of *"Mitte! Mitte!"*—"Let him go! Let him go!" On the other hand, spectators might shout, *"Iugula!"*—"Cut his throat!" If the emperor was present, the decision of life or death was left in his hands, although he usually deferred to the wishes of the crowd.

For variety's sake, the *procurators*, or managers, might arrange especially exotic matches. Dwarfs matched with women, women against women, or blacks against blacks always appealed to the crowd. Occasionally an especially skilled female gladiator might fight a male. One woman, named Stratonici, won fame by killing three men in a row while she was armed only with a metal chamber pot. For this performance she won her freedom and a state pension for the rest of her life.

Like Stratonici, most gladiators were not free. They either had been purchased for the purpose from the slave markets or were prisoners of war. The few who volunteered for the arena, lured by either a sense of adventure or a desire for the prize money, signed a contract with a *lanista*, a professional gladiator trainer, to fight for a specific period of time. Successful gladiators, whether slave or free, became instant celebrities, commanding the same type of public homage as professional sports figures do today.

These brutal fights, or *munera*, were interspersed during the day with special beast fights called *venationes*. In these grisly contests, bestiarii fought a variety of exotic animals imported from throughout the Empire. Elephants, lions, hippos, rhinos, buffalo, and tigers were killed by the thousands throughout the imperial period for the amusement of the Roman crowd. The Roman poet Marcus Valerius Martialis (A.D. 40–104), known as Martial, wrote glowingly about a wild sow whose belly was cut open during a fight by a bestiarius, releasing a baby pig to run squealing around the arena. Martial found the occurrence original and exciting and compared it to the mythological birth of the god Bacchus, who was cut from his mother's womb when she died.

The number of people and animals killed for the amusement of a bored but potentially fickle and dangerous crowd staggers the imagination. To celebrate his victories in Dacia (roughly, modern Moldova and Romania), for example, the emperor Trajan treated the people to 123 straight days of gladiatorial combat, during which ten thousand men fought and half that many died. When Vespasian's son Titus (r. A.D. 79–81) dedicated the Colosseum in June 80, five thousand wild animals were butchered in a single day. Romans, as we do today, waged war on the environment. The intensive hunting of animals for arenas throughout the Empire brought about the wholesale destruction of animal species from extensive areas. Roman animal catchers eliminated the lion from the Middle East, the tiger from northern Iran, the hippopotamus from Nubia, and the elephant from North Africa.

TITUS

Vespasian's prosperous and otherwise peaceful regime continued under both his sons. The first, Titus Flavius Vespasianus, despite a dissipated youth, became as serious and industrious as his father and maintained his father's policies. His short reign, however, was

The Early Empire

marred by three significant natural disasters. On August 24, 79, Mount Vesuvius, which overlooked the resort cities of Pompeii and Herculaneum just south of Naples in Campania in southern Italy, began to erupt; the next day a superheated cloud of gas, pumice, and ash hurtled downhill at sixty miles an hour (96.5kph) and buried both cities.

The same year, a plague swept through Campania, and in 80, fire engulfed Rome for three days, destroying or severely damaging temples and private homes. Titus, who seems to have held himself responsible for these disasters, donated lavishly to a relief fund for the survivors. He died on September 1, 80, exclaiming, with his last breath, that he thought it unjust that the Roman people should have suffered so much misery because of "a single sin." He never revealed, nor has anyone ever discovered, what that "sin" was. A few of his contemporaries believed he was referring to an incestuous liason with his brother's wife, Domitia, but Domitia, an infamous libertine, emphatically denied any such relationship although she brazenly admitted to numerous others.

DOMITIAN

His brother, Titus Flavius Domitianus (r. 81–96), succeeded Titus, and though his personal conduct was certainly not as restrained as that of his brother and father, he maintained their policies and the Empire continued to prosper. During his reign, Domitian defeated a rebellion by the Roman governor of Germany and an invasion by barbarian tribes from Dacia. He won the devotion of his soldiers by personally leading the Roman armies as they drove the invaders back across the Danube.

Throughout his reign, Domitian always found the resources to endear himself to the Roman people with extravagant shows and building programs. He completed the Colosseum and the public baths begun by Titus and restored the Pantheon, the Baths of Agrippa, and the Temples of Serapis and Isis that had been damaged by the fire of 80. He also built an impressive temple to his father, plus another temple to *Jupiter* Custos (the Guardian). His greatest monument, however, was the great Temple of *Jupiter Optimus Maximus*, atop the Capitoline, with its gilt roof and gold-plated doors. Despite these expenditures, when Domitian died in 96, the state treasury was full, a tribute to the fiscal reforms of his father and his own considerable financial ability.

During the last years of his reign, Domitian fell victim to paranoia, striking out blindly at anyone he imagined was plotting against him. In quick succession he ordered the arrest and execution of Roman governors in Britain, Asia, and Egypt; the commander of the Praetorian Guard; and his own grandnephew Flavius Clemens and his wife, Flavia Domitilla, on a charge of impiety. The historian Dio Cassius (c. A.D. 150–235) claimed the couple's "impiety" was a form of Judaism, and this has led many scholars to assume they might have been Christians. If this is correct, it corroborates the recent research of the sociologist Rodney Stark, who maintains that Christianity did not initially develop among the poor and disposed, as Christian legend holds, but among the wealthy and middle classes.

As Domitian's paranoia grew, he hung mirrors along the palace corridors where he walked for exercise so that he could always see who was behind him. To emphasize the point that there could be absolutely no justification for killing an emperor, he ordered the execution of Nero's faithful freedman, Epaphroditus, who had reluctantly killed Nero at that emperor's express order. Domitian's suspicions finally extended to his wife, Domitia, who upon learning that her husband suspected her acted preemptively, persuading the imperial butler, Stephanus, to stab Domitian in his bedroom.

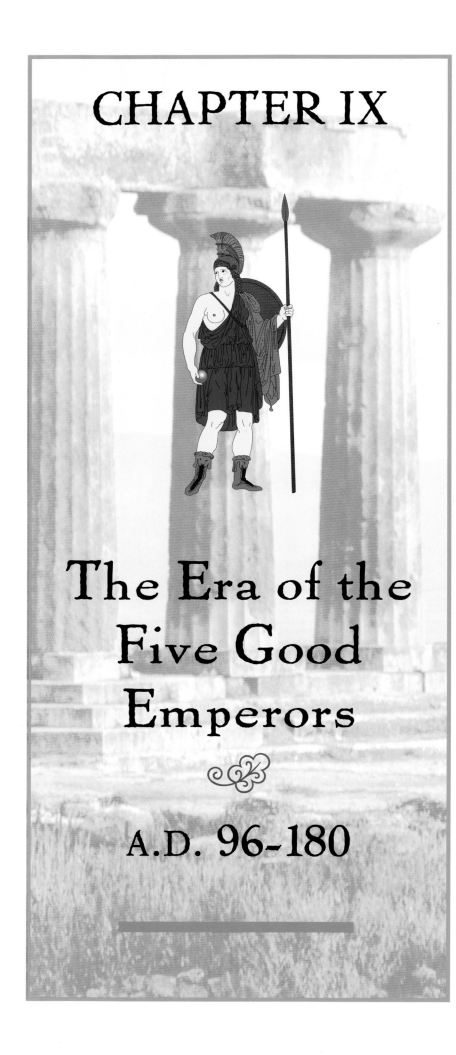

CHAPTER IX

The Era of the Five Good Emperors

A.D. 96-180

IN THE FIRST PARAGRAPH of his *Decline and Fall of the Roman Empire*, the English historian Edward Gibbon writes that the years between 96 and 180 constituted the most secure and civilized period in European history up to and including his own time. The borders of the Empire were secure, the army was well disciplined, the rule of law was respected throughout the Empire, the economy was robust, the Roman Constitution protected the rights of individual citizens, and the Roman Senate, in conjunction with the emperors, ruled wisely and well. Two centuries of historical research since the 1776 publication of Gibbon's massive study have in the main supported his rosy picture of a society at its apex.

the Senate, demonstrating his deep respect for that body by recalling exiled senators, promising publicly never to execute a senator who had not been condemned by the Senate, and repealing the hated *maiestas minuta populi Romani*, a law that had been much abused since it was passed in 103 B.C. Literally "reducing the dignity of the Roman people," it could be interpreted to condemn any senator's behavior, from making a joke about the emperor to organizing a full-scale rebellion. Emperors from Tiberius on had used the law to rid themselves of their senatorial enemies. Nerva's repeal of this unpopular law made the Senate happy.

During his short reign, Nerva instituted some wise reforms, including financial ones that improved the economy of Rome and of Italy. He ensured the honesty of the officials collecting taxes and implemented innovative financial measures, including establishing a fund to lend money to Italian farmers experiencing financial difficulties. The goverment used the interest these farmers paid—generally 5 percent—to care for needy girls and boys.

MARCUS COCCEIUS NERVA

Immediately after the murder of Domitian, the Senate appointed Marcus Cocceius Nerva emperor. The senators were able to do this because they had paid a generous sum to the Praetorian Guard and because Domitian's death was so unexpected that there was nobody to challenge their decision.

Nerva, sixty years old at the time of his ascension, was noted for his complaisant nature and his esteem for the Senate, of which he was a member. His affability and tact—not to mention his gift for survival—are evidenced by the fact that he had been a confidant of both Nero and Domitian. Once in power, Nerva cultivated

TRAJAN

Few people expected Nerva to live long, and the Senate in particular encouraged him to name a successor; he chose Marcus Ulpius Trajanus, a distinguished general who was also acceptable to the Senate. During Trajan's reign, the Empire would reach its greatest extent while continuing to enjoy virtually

uninterrupted peace and prosperity. The emperors were clearly dictators, since the Senate never seriously challenged their power, yet under Trajan and his immediate successors the Empire seemed to manifest many of the characteristics of the old Republic. Behind it all, however, was the sure hand of the emperor, making his will known indirectly to key senators with the assurance that it would be done.

Trajan advertised his power as all rulers do, with a flurry of construction in Rome and elsewhere. He made improvements in the harbor at Ostia, undertook flood-control projects, built elaborate public baths, and—his crowning achievement—built a magnificent forum to relieve the crowded conditions in the other forums in Rome. Trajan's Forum was larger than any other,

measuring 1017 by 606 feet (310 by 185m), with beautifully designed porticoes on three sides. In the center was an equestrian statue of the emperor that was cast in bronze. At the north end of the open forum was the *basilica Ulpia*, named for the emperor's family, an elaborate covered building in which public business could be conducted. Next to the outside north wall of the basilica were two marble libraries, the *bibliothecae* Ulpiae; framed between the entrances of the libraries was Trajan's magnificent column.

The column still stands ninety-five feet (29m) high atop a twenty-foot (6m) pedestal. An internal spiral staircase winds up to a platform at the top, where an eagle stood until 1588, when Pope Sixtus V (1585–90) ordered it removed and replaced with a statue of Saint

The Era of the Five Good Emperors

Peter. On the outside surface of the pillar, circling from bottom to top, is a carved helical band of sculpture, 656 feet (200m) long and up to $4^{3}/_{4}$ feet (1.5m) wide, a pictorial history of Trajan's conquest of Dacia between A.D. 101 and 105. It is a seamless example of art in the service of propaganda.

There is no comparable artistic innovation to commemorate Trajan's equally impressive conquest of Parthia, an event that ended for nearly a quarter century the military threat from the east. The war was ignited by Parthian interference in the internal affairs of Armenia, an independent kingdom but one that Rome considered vital to her interests, and ended with the Roman capture of Ctesiphon, the Parthian capital on the Tigris. This conquest enabled Trajan to add to the Empire a portion of Mesopotamia that reached all the way to the head of the Persian Gulf.

He even thought briefly of sending Roman armies to India.

Despite the glory of the war against Parthia, Trajan had in reality expanded the borders of the Empire beyond the ability of the Roman military and administrative system to defend and support. The effort had also taken a toll on Trajan himself, whose health was ruined in the three-year desert campaign. In 116, he became ill and returned to Antioch from Ctesiphon. Unable to shake his illness, he began the journey back to Rome but died on the way, at Silinus in southern Turkey in August 117. When word of his death reached his army in Antioch, the troops immediately proclaimed his second-in-command, Publius Aelius Hadrianus, emperor. When the Senate in Rome learned of this, they meekly accepted the soldiers' decision.

Constructing an Empire

Throughout Hadrian's travels he spent lavishly, building temples and public buildings. In 128, for instance, during a trip to Athens, he ordered the construction of various temples, a gymnasium, a library, and a stoa, or covered walkway, as his personal tribute to the city he felt was still the cultural capital of the world. Nor did he confine his construction to foreign cities. Two of his most famous projects in Rome were his building his own mausoleum (today Castel Sant'Angelo) and his rebuilding of the Pantheon.

Originally built by Augustus' advisor Agrippa to serve as a temple to all the gods, the Pantheon burned in the Great Fire during Titus' reign, leaving only the front portico bearing Agrippa's inscription atop sixteen Corinthian pillars. Hadrian had this singular monument rebuilt on a grand scale. Today, it is a circular building with an interior diameter of 132 feet (40m). Its walls are twenty feet (6m) thick to support the massive dome that crowns the building and allows in the only natural light through a round opening 30 feet (9.1m) in diameter at the top of the dome. Its massive bronze doors are original.

If this wonder of harmonious architectural proportions has survived, it is not by chance but because the Catholic Church adopted the Pantheon as a church in 609. The coffered dome has served as the model for similar structures throughout the world, most notably Saint Peter's Church in Rome and the United States Capitol in Washington, D.C.

HADRIAN

Hadrian's rule was even more successful than Trajan's, chiefly because the Empire did not have to pay for any long, expensive wars—with the single, significant exception of the revolt in Judea. In October 131, a Jewish guerrilla leader, Bar Kokhba, led an insurrection, provoked by Hadrian's plan to establish a Roman colony in Judea and by several of the emperor's measures. These included a ban on the practice of circumcision, which the Romans felt was barbaric but was crucial to Jewish religious practice; an imperial edict prohibiting Jews from entering Jerusalem more than once a year; and Hadrian's building a pagan temple on the site of the Jewish temple. Bar Kokhba and his fighters nearly captured Jerusalem, threatening the Roman hold on Judea and requiring Hadrian to send one of his best generals, Gaius Julius Severus, to defeat the rebels. It took four years, during which time Severus fragmented the country and starved a large number of Jews to death. The revolt did not end, however, until Bar Kokhba was hunted down and killed.

Otherwise, Hadrian's policy throughout the Empire was defensive. The most famous of the walls he built to guard the Empire is the one today called Hadrian's Wall in Britain. He also fortified the area in southern Germany between the Rhine and Danube Rivers with towers and walled camps. Most consequential, though, was his realization that the Roman occupation of Mesopotamia was beyond her ability to maintain. He withdrew the legions in that area westward to a more defensible frontier.

Hadrian was also aware that the best guarantee of efficiency and security within the Empire was the personal attention of the emperor; as a result he spent nearly twelve years of his twenty-one-year reign on tours of inspection throughout the Roman world, visiting everything from major cities to small garrisons to outposts. From 121 to 126, Hadrian visited Gaul, Britain, Germany, Spain, and distant Mauretania in northwestern Africa. Between 128 and 134, he visited the eastern part of the Empire including Asia Minor,

Right: Hadrian's Wall stretched all the way across England from Newcastle to Carlisle, marking the northern limit of effective Roman control. For purposes of security, however, the Romans built fortresses north of the wall to act as additional frontier security positions. Here a modern farmer has cut a gate in a remnant of the wall and utilizes it as a cattle fence.

The Era of the Five Good Emperors

Greece, and Egypt. He developed the habit of suddenly appearing at trouble spots to take charge of problems. His unexpected arrival in 128 at Ephesus, on the coast of Asia Minor, discouraged the Parthians from attacking the Roman frontier on the Euphrates River, and they settled for renegotiating their treaty with Rome.

PROTECTING THE PEOPLE

Hadrian cared even for the lowliest inhabitants of the Empire. Everywhere he went he showed compassion for the poor, lifting taxes where there had been famine or other natural disasters, freezing prices for basic foods, and encouraging cultivation of marginal lands by giving settlers economic incentives to make improvements.

However, his chief concern was for the army, for he realized that it guaranteed both the internal and external security of the Empire as well as his own survival. He made numerous changes that improved the lot of the common soldier; one of his most popular measures changed the existing laws to allow garrisoned soldiers to live with women in nearby towns. Another permitted soldiers to make wills leaving their property to their children. While it was still illegal for the common soldier to marry, these changes acknowledged what was already happening illegally and made the army a more attractive career.

Continuing one of Trajan's reforms, Hadrian began recruiting special troops called *numeri*, local men who joined the army without undergoing the special training for legionnaires that stressed fighting in the rigid formations that were the mainstay of the Roman army. These troops, many of them cavalry and mounted archers from Mesopotamia, were allowed to arm and fight according to their local customs. They were not assigned to their home areas but were distributed around the Empire's frontiers, a kind of mobile reserve to back up the heavy legions of the permanent garrisons. In the two centuries after Hadrian, these troops evolved into the heavy cavalry units that would prove so effective in blocking barbarian breakthroughs along the borders.

Hadrian also took the unprecedented step of stationing a legion in Italy at Albanum, near Rome, intended as a mobile reserve that could be dispatched to any part of the border that might be threatened by invaders. The Senate, however, feared that the legion might be used to intimidate them.

THE SENATE

Despite—or because of—his popularity with the army, Hadrian never got on well with the Senate, although they never directly challenged him. Their concern was that Hadrian might be slowly eroding senatorial power while preserving an outward appearance of congeniality and submission.

Hadrian appointed new senators from throughout the Empire, so by the end of his reign the Senate was truly representative of the Empire as a whole. This, of course, angered

the old senatorial families, whose roots in that legislative body went back centuries. Hadrian also continued to appoint to the government administrative officials who were drawn from the middle class.

Most imperial of Hadrian's acts was his designation of his heir; Hadrian was the first emperor to name his successor during his lifetime. As he had no sons, he adopted a close friend, Lucius Ceionius Commodus Verus, as his son and successor. After this man died in 138, Hadrian adopted Titus Aurelius Antoninus and named him heir, also designating the sixteen-year-old Marcus Annius Verus second in line. In time, both men became emperors under the names, respectively, of Antoninus Pius (r. 138–161) and Marcus Aurelius (r. 161–180).

ANTONINUS PIUS

Antoninus Pius' chief claim to fame was the peace and prosperity that characterized his reign. The frontiers were untroubled, the Empire was free of revolts, and no major natural disasters caused suffering or challenged the Empire's economic stability. Antoninus Pius was therefore able to spend much of his time in bucolic pursuits, two of his favorite being feeding chickens on his estate at Lorium in northern Campania and hunting.

Yet he had impressive intellectual gifts, especially in law. It was as a successful jurist that Antoninus had first caught Hadrian's attention, so it was only natural that during his reign Antoninus should stress the study of law. With a panel of fellow jurists, the emperor prepared commentaries on Roman law while himself codifying and summarizing the laws on inheritance, trusts, and the legal rights of minors.

As the chief source of new law within the Empire, Antoninus did much to pass more humane laws for large segments of the Roman population. As was customary, he forgave taxes for areas that had suffered famine, earthquake, plague, or other afflictions. In addition, his laws prosecuted masters who killed their slaves, gave slaves legal recourse for harsh treatment by their masters, limited imprisonment in the mines to ten years, granted Jews the right of circumcision, and established the legal precedent that a prisoner was innocent until proven guilty and, further, that in the event of a tie vote by the judges, the prisoner was freed.

Like his more conscientious predecessors, Antoninus tried to get along with both the Senate and the people of Rome. He made it a point to treat the Senate with respect, attend their meetings, and consult with leading senators. He won the allegiance

of the people by building public baths and improving the harbor facilities at Ostia, thus helping to ensure an adequate supply of grain for Rome. He also spent lavishly on public games. His sound fiscal policies resulted in a surplus in the state treasury of 2,700,000,000 sesterces when he died.

In foreign affairs, his preference for settling problems with diplomacy rather than force inadvertently created a problem, for the legions began to lose their edge. In an age of warfare, where results depended on the shock effect of blade against blade, soldiers had to maintain a high level of training and physical fitness. The peaceful conditions at the frontiers, however, eroded the need for training—a fact that was not lost on the Germanic and Celtic tribes across the border. These tribes took advantage of relaxed relations to observe Roman civilization, adopt Roman weapons, and learn Roman tactics. The lack of rigorous military discipline would nearly prove the undoing of the Empire after Antoninus' death, when hundreds of thousands of Germans swarmed across the Danube at the same time that the Parthians were attacking Roman border garrisons along the Euphrates River.

MARCUS AURELIUS

Fortunately for the Empire, Antoninus' successor was one of the greatest emperors that Rome ever produced. Marcus Aurelius, like Trajan and Hadrian before him, was of Spanish descent, although he had been born and raised in Rome. Unlike those two emperors, he received the best education available and excelled in rhetoric, that is, effective writing and public speaking, and philosophy; he is recalled as one of the great Stoic thinkers and writers. He desired above all else a life of contemplation and intellectual debate, but his sense of civic responsibility was greater still. Upon the death of

Antoninus Pius, Marcus Aurelius took the unprecedented step of requesting Lucius Verus as coemperor.

In 161, the first year of his reign, Marcus Aurelius was thrust into one of the Empire's greatest moments of crisis when the Parthian king Vologeses invaded Armenia and threatened the stability of the Syrian-Mesopotamian frontier. Lucius Verus hurried to the area and with two experienced generals, Ovidius Cassius and Status Priscus, overwhelmed the Parthian forces in Armenia and Mesopotamia. By 165, the Roman army had penetrated to Ctesiphon, the Parthian capital, and was on the point of exterminating the Parthian forces when their army was ravaged by smallpox. The disease, which caused the Romans to fall back to their own frontier, decimated both sides, preventing a successful Parthian counterattack. The Romans were able to conclude a peace treaty in the region.

The returning Roman army brought the disease back to Italy, where it killed up to one-third of the population. To compound this disaster, two Germanic tribes, the Quasi and the Marcomanni, joined later by a Sarmatian tribe, the Iazyges, crossed the Danube and the Alps, penetrating as far as the shores of the Adriatic Sea, where they laid siege to the port city of Aquileia. A little later, another group of Sarmatians, the Costoboci, broke through the Roman defenses on the lower Danube, drove deep into the Balkan peninsula, and nearly took Athens.

Marcus Aurelius was suddenly thrust into a role for which few thought him fit but in which he flourished. With many of his troops felled by disease, he gathered together a scratch force of veterans, slaves, gladiators, and freed convicts, molded them into an army, and hurried north to meet the challenge. In a number of pitched battles he forced the barbarians back, lifted the siege of Aquileia, and pushed the invaders back across the

The Era of the Five Good Emperors

The Persecution of the Christians

Marcus Aurelius' philosophical emphasis on personal morality and public ethics seems to stand in contradiction to the fierce persecution of Christians that took place during his reign. While no surviving document indicates his specific orders in this regard, ancient Christian authors such as Eusebius (263–339), bishop of the early Christian community of Caesarea (modern Qisarya, near Haifa, Israel), report persecutions by Roman officials during his reign.

The answer to why so rational and ethical an emperor at least countenanced persecution of the small, nonviolent Christian minority lies perhaps in the period's atmosphere of extreme crisis. All at once and everywhere, Roman society appeared to be menaced by barbarian invaders, famine, disease, and internal disloyalty. What held the Empire together was a veneration for the gods—the Romans had embraced a number of "foreign" deities, such as Isis—and the emperor, himself officially considered divine. This the Christians publicly refused to do. To get some inkling of the reaction of Roman citizens to this refusal, it is only necessary to remember the anger that many in the United States felt during the Vietnam War toward fellow citizens who refused to salute the American flag.

Certain misconceptions about Christianity were prevalent among even educated Romans—the most likely to influence the emperor. For instance, Marcus Cornelius Fronto (95–166), an internationally respected intellectual and the emperor's rhetoric tutor when he was a boy, stated in a letter that Christians performed impious and immoral acts, such as consecrating and worshiping the head of a donkey, habitually committing incest, and clubbing infants to death, after which they would dismember the bodies, drink the blood, and eat the limbs. Some Christian practices in fact reinforced these misconceptions; for example, the early Church, even in periods without persecution, met secretly, which was sure to arouse suspicion, especially in a time of upheaval.

An 1888 color lithograph depicts the persecution of Christians in Rome at the Circus Maximus. Persecution of the Christians, who were largely regarded as antisocial and unpatriotic, varied from reign to reign, but was most extreme in times of unrest. The secret meetings of the Christians only fueled pagans' suspicions of the new religion, and rumors of infanticide, blood sacrifices, and other unsavory practices added to the distrust.

Danube. Then, at the moment of victory, smallpox broke out among his army once more, forcing Marcus Aurelius to sign a peace treaty with the invaders. To compound the Empire's troubles, Ovidius Cassius, the governor of Syria, rebelled, and it seemed that the Parthians might reopen an attack on the Empire.

As Marcus Aurelius moved east to meet these challenges, disaster struck him personally when his beloved wife, Faustina, mother of his four children, died in 175. Perhaps he found comfort in his Stoic philosophy, which taught that all objects and events in the universe share a common essence and are inter-related by fate, which in the Stoic system is a web of cause and effect. During his many campaigns, Marcus Aurelius kept a "spiritual diary," later published as his *Meditations*, which gives insight into the balance he attempted to maintain between his philosophical convictions and his worldly duties. He expressed his belief in writings such as "Whatever happens at all happens as it should; you will find this true, if you watch narrowly."

By 178, he was back at the Danube, fighting the Marcomanni and Quasi again. He crushed them in a series of quick campaigns and annexed the territory that now composes Bavaria, north of the river, to create a buffer. He planned to advance the frontier to the Carpathian Mountains, thereby establishing a defensible frontier along their crest, but in March 180, he himself succumbed to smallpox and died.

The unexpected death of Marcus Aurelius in 180 and the ruinous costs of his many campaigns to contain an increasingly indefensible Empire brought a sudden halt to a long period of prosperity and well-being in the Empire. The successful balance of a relatively decentralized imperial administration and a single, powerful leader would shortly begin to fail. As long as

the borders of the Empire went unchallenged and the emperor was an enlightened administrator, Rome enjoyed stability, peace, and prosperity. The human cost of maintaining the social order at times seems unacceptably high by today's standards but perhaps seemed less so compared with the chaos of the civil wars during the period of the Republic

By the same token, when so much power was in the hands of a single man who was unfit for it, the consequences were devastating. After 180, the office of emperor began more and more to be held by weak, ineffective rulers who lacked character, strength, and intelligence. Ironically, Marcus Aurelius' own son, Lucius Aelius Aurelius Commodus, proved to be an irresponsible libertine and general reprobate who destroyed everything his father had fought so hard to pre-serve. Over the next three hundred years, while there would occasionally be men who stemmed its political, economic, and military decline, the Empire grew steadily more feeble. This process of degeneration was accelerated by the unremitting pressure of hundreds of thou-sands of barbarian invaders at the "gates" of the Empire.

The Era of the Five Good Emperors

CHAPTER X

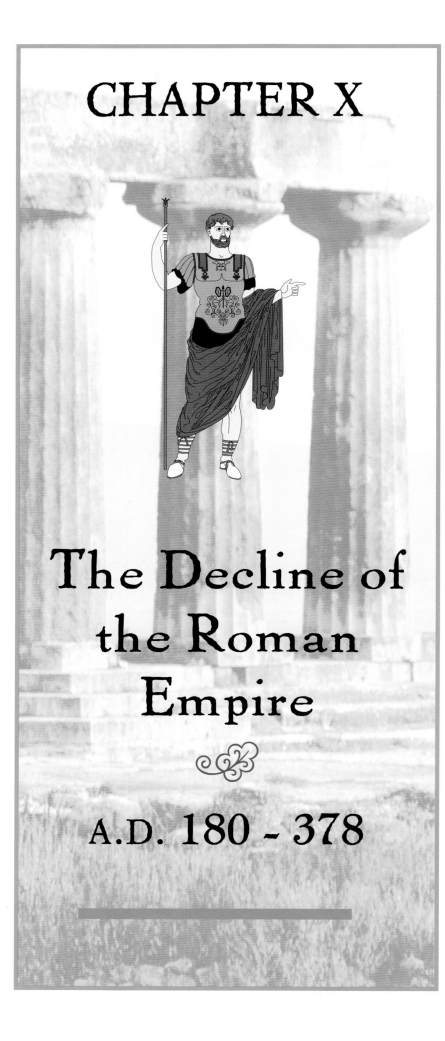

The Decline of the Roman Empire

❧

A.D. 180 - 378

FOR FIFTEEN HUNDRED years now, one of the most popular activities among historians of Europe has been speculating about the reasons for the sudden collapse of the Empire of the west in A.D. 476. In that year, the Germanic leader Odoacer deposed Romulus Augustulus (known as the last Roman emperor), pensioned him off in a monastery in Campania, and abolished the office and title of emperor. In eastern Europe and Asia Minor, the Byzantine Empire survived for another eleven hundred years with the brilliant city of Constantinople as its capital. That empire only ended in May 1453, when Mohammed II, sultan of the Ottoman Empire, took the city and changed its name to Istanbul.

The reasons that historians through the ages have given for the fall of the Roman Empire often reflect their own attitudes and biases as well as those of their times. Soon after the fall itself, both pagans and Christians maintained that the Empire had disintegrated because of impiety, but while the pagans believed this meant that Rome had abandoned the old gods, the Catholic and Orthodox Christians felt that too many were still worshiping them—or else practicing unacceptable forms of Christianity.

Through subsequent centuries, other reasons have been put forward. Victorian historians tended to cite a decline in morals as the cause for the Empire's decline. More recently, in the 1960s, fundamentalist Christians blamed homosexuality, while environmentalists speculated that abrupt climatic changes created a series of food shortages that precipitated the Empire's collapse.

In the 1970s a popular explanation was that accidental lead poisoning compromised the fertility of the upper classes. The theory is that because the Romans lacked the means to seal their wine containers (they had no knowledge of corks), Roman wine was drunk young. To mellow the astringent new wine, upper-class Romans had it heated in lead-lined containers; in the process, the lead leached into the wine. Since it was the upper class that produced the capable rulers, Rome was left with an inferior population from which to draw its future leaders.

A further ecological argument of the 1970s attributed the end of the Roman Empire to soil erosion due to the overcultivation of farm land, resulting in an Empire-wide loss of valuable top soil. The western part of the Empire would thus have been obliged to import food from the eastern; this imbalance of trade would ultimately have bankrupted the western half.

While some of these imaginative theories propose factors that contributed to the decline and fall of the Roman Empire, no one of them describes circumstances that were unique to the Empire of the west. Any one of these trends was true at one time or another of the eastern part of the Empire as well— which continued for more than a millennium. Of all the events that affected the Roman Empire in the nearly three hundred years between 180 and 476, only the barbarian invasions were specific to the west.

THE ENEMY AT THE GATES

From the late second century A.D. Germanic invaders, whom the Romans termed barbarians, attempted to

breach the borders of the eastern part of the Empire. They failed to make any lasting gains because of the strategic position of Constantinople itself. Set on its peninsula jutting into the sea, and protected on the land side by three massive rings of walls, the city was virtually impregnable to a land attack. Furthermore, a powerful fleet prevented any significant penetration into the Asian territories of the Empire because the barbarian peoples lacked naval capabilities.

In the west, however, repeated barbarian attacks in the same period created a chronic military and economic strain that eventually simply exhausted the Empire's resources. The surprising thing is not that the Empire fell in 476, but that it lasted for nearly three hundred years under this unremitting pressure.

Before the time of Marcus Aurelius, the barbarian border raids tended to threaten only one part of the Empire's border at a time. But during Aurelius' reign the attacks were occurring all along the frontier. Before, commanders could shift their troops to meet any localized threat, so a comparatively small army had long been adequate. During Marcus Aurelius'

reign, however, and forever after, multiple attacks over an extended area strained the Empire's defenses. By the late third century A.D. Rome increased the size of the army to about half a million men, a figure that was difficult for its economy to support.

The army, long a key element in Roman politics, now moved to center stage. Supporting it became the Empire's single most important economic goal and its generals its most important political players. The Senate became a tool of the generals. The new reality was reflected in the dying words of the emperor Septimius Severus (r. 193–211) to his sons: "Enrich the soldiers; ignore everyone else."

THE LEGACY OF MARCUS AURELIUS

Marcus Aurelius was succeeded by his son, Lucius Aelius Aurelius Commodus (r. 180–192), whom the emperor had made coruler in 177, but Commodus had learned little. Bored with the war on the Danube, Commodus made a disastrous peace with the Germanic tribes in order to hurry back to Rome to enjoy the pleasures of absolute rule. He filled a harem with three hundred of the most beautiful women in Rome and another with three hundred of the handsomest young men, dividing his time between the two. He loved the games, trained as a gladiator, and then, vain about his physical prowess, entertained the populace of Rome by fighting in the arena.

Although he engaged in 750 duels against gladiators, these could hardly be considered fair fights; in

Left: A barbarian fights a Roman, second century A.D. This stone relief, now in the Louvre of Paris, shows why initially the Romans, although outnumbered so often, beat barbarian invaders: the Romans had standardized armor, while the barbarians did not. In the background stands a barbarian hut.

the first place, he was the emperor, and in the second, while he used conventional weapons, he armed his opponents with soft lead ones. He was an expert archer and once killed one hundred lions with one hundred arrows; a consummate showman, he designed special arrows with crescent-shaped tips, which he then used to cut off the heads of one hundred ostriches—to the delight of the spectators. Commodus' athletic skill convinced him that he was the reincarnation of Hercules, so in imitation of his hero, he took to wandering the streets of Rome clad in a lionskin and carrying a huge club.

Preoccupied with his own interests and activities, Commodus left the affairs of state in the hands of his favorites, then simply had them killed when they became too powerful. The last of them, Laetus, fearing that the time for his own murder was drawing near, conspired with Commodus' mistress, Marcia, to kill him. Marcia drugged Commodus and smuggled a professional wrestler into the palace who then strangled him.

The results were predictable. Immediately, three claimants in separate parts of the Empire declared themselves emperor, and civil war broke out. On January 1, 193, the Praetorian Guard and the Senate declared one of them, Publius Helvius Pertinax, emperor, but when Pertinax attempted to reform the finances of the Empire, he angered both the general population and the army. Sixty-eight days after Pertinax was proclaimed emperor, the Praetorian Guard murdered him.

The Praetorian Guard, holding the power to make emperors, put the office up for public auction.

Two senators, Didius Julianus and his father-in-law, Sulpicianus, engaged in a bidding match for the Empire. Julianus won with an offer to pay the fifteen thousand Praetorians twenty-five thousand sesterces each. The civil war continued, however, and by June 1, 193, one of the contenders, Septimius Severus, proclaimed emperor by his troops, had fought his way to Rome. Julianus killed himself after a reign of only sixty-six days.

SEPTIMIUS SEVERUS

Septimius Severus was a gifted ruler who, well aware of the army's importance, made changes instrumental in the army's ability to hold back the invaders for the next seventy years. He reformed the Praetorian Guard, which until then had recruited only Italians, so that this crucial unit might draw upon the best soldiers from throughout the Empire. He likewise opened the highest ranks to individuals on the basis of merit rather than birth or family connections. In the future, men who had entered the army as simple legionnaires could advance to become emperor.

Septimius' administrative reforms took the last vestiges of power from the Senate. No longer using the Senate as a council, he created instead an Imperial Council, whose members were appointed by himself. He relieved senators of their governmental functions in Rome and turned most of their duties over to the praetorian prefect. Professional jurists replaced the

Left: A rock sculpture depicts the victory of Sapor I (r. 240–272) over the emperor Valerian (r. 253–260), the only Roman emperor captured in battle. He ended his life as a hostage at the court of Sapor, who enjoyed humiliating him and often used him as a stepping stool for mounting a horse. Here the defeated emperor kneels before Sapor seated on his horse.

senators who had previously acted as judges, and Septimius confiscated the estates of any senators who spoke up against his trumped-up charges of treason.

Septimius' military decisions were sometimes those of a general, not an emperor. For example, when he continued the war against the Parthians, he not only took their capital at Ctesiphon but re-created the province of Mesopotamia, which Hadrian had abandoned more than fifty years before. The Parthian adventure had two disastrous consequences. First, it so destabilized the Parthian government that it was eventually replaced by a much more aggressive dynasty, the Sasanids, who would prove to be a much more active enemy than Rome had ever had to face on the eastern frontier. Second, the province of Mesopotamia was strategically impossible to defend, yet demanded a great many soldiers and resources.

Despite his policy in the east, Septimius Severus was an efficient, if sometimes tyrannical, ruler. After his death in 211 during a campaign in Britain, the Empire entered a seventy-three-year period of chaos that was dominated by emperors who were either incompetent or, if competent, were murdered before they could stem the erosion of the Empire. Some of the statistics concerning this period are truly staggering.

Between the death of Septimius Severus and the beginning of Diocletian's reign in 284, there were twenty-seven emperors. Seventeen were murdered—sixteen by their own troops; two committed suicide to avoid execution at the hands of a successful rival; three died in battle; and one was captured by the Sasanids. Only four died in their beds.

THE REIGN OF CHAOS

The Empire was coming apart at the frontiers, where barbarian tribes were striking deep into the territories of the Empire. In 267 and 268, Goths sacked Ephesus in Asia Minor and Athens. In 253, the Alemanni invaded Italy, raiding the countryside around Rome at the same time that another Germanic tribe, the Franks, were storming Gaul and northern Spain. Between 230 and 253, the Sasanids overran Syria, southern Asia Minor, and Armenia.

In 256, the Sasanid king, Sapor I, captured the emperor Valerian (r. 253–260) in battle near Edessa. Sapor took Valerian back to his capital, where he periodically forced the defeated emperor to crouch on all fours to provide a footstool for Sapor to use to mount his horse. Nor was defeat confined to the east. In 270, one of the few effective rulers of the period, Aurelian

(r. 270–275), unable to withstand the barbarian incursions, was forced to cede the province of Dacia and to withdraw the frontier to the Danube River.

In the mid-third century A.D. plague—either smallpox or measles—struck the Empire with devastating effects. In Rome, it took the lives of as many as five thousand people in a single day; more than 60 percent of the people in Alexandria died. Even emperors were not immune, and in 270 the epidemic killed the current emperor, Claudius Gothicus (one of those who died in his bed). Pestilence and defeat on the battlefields created a serious manpower shortage in the Roman army, and the emperors were increasingly obliged to allow barbarian tribes to settle within the Empire along the frontiers in return for their enrollment in the Roman army.

The emperor Probus (r. 276–282) defeated the Germans in Gaul but permitted seventy thousand of them to settle within the Empire, thus acquiring sixteen thousand soldiers. Later, when he defeated the

The Changing Face of the Empire

In the disorder of the third century, various regional leaders within the Empire broke away from Rome to form their own empires. In part due to the central government's inability to defend these regions from invasion or civil war, these independence movements were at times expressions of incipient or regained nationalisms.

One regional leader, Marcus Cassianius Latinus Postumus, originally a general commanding Roman forces in Gaul under the emperor Publius Licinius Egnatius Gallienus (253–268), revolted in 260, hoping to use the confusion surrounding the capture of Valerian to establish a "Gallic Empire," composed of Gaul, Spain, and Britain. For nine years—until he was assassinated by his own troops, who did not feel they were adequately rewarded—he maintained his Empire, drove back several Germanic invasions, and even issued his own coinage.

Septimius Odaenathus, with his queen, Zenobia, ruled Palmyra, a caravan city in southern Syria. He took advantage of the disorder surrounding the capture of Valerian to make a bid for independence. He defeated the Sasanid ruler, Sapor I, and drove the Sasanids out of Armenia and Mesopotamia.

Odaenathus died mysteriously in 267. Some believe that Zenobia murdered him because she succeeded her husband in the name of their son, Septimius Vaballathus. Her armies captured Egypt and three-quarters of Asia Minor before the emperor Aurelian defeated her armies and captured her. Dramatically, he brought her back to Rome and forced her to march behind his chariot in golden chains in his triumph, but instead of having her strangled—the usual fate of captured rulers—he pensioned her off in a villa in Tivoli, where she married a senator and became just another Roman matron.

Dating from the first half of the first century A.D., these figures represent the Palmyrean Triad, the gods Aglibol, Baalshamin, and Malakbel (left to right). They once stood in Palmyra (now central Syria), the capital of the kingdom ruled by King Odaenathus (r. 250–267) and later by his beautiful queen Zenobia (240?–300?), whose rule ended in 273 when the emperor Aurelian (r. 270–275) captured the city.

Scythians along the lower Danube, he admitted 100,000 men, women, and children into the Empire. The twenty-five thousand Scythians served with distinction well into the fourth century. These "immigrants" proved to be effective soldiers who not only readily adapted to Roman command but also brought into Roman military practice their traditional tactics. Fears that they might betray the Empire to other barbarians across the borders proved groundless: in the entire subsequent military history of the western part of the Empire, not one instance of such collusion was ever reported.

THE COLLAPSE OF THE ROMAN ECONOMY

The by-now chronic problems of defense on the frontier had created a severe financial drain on the Empire. In order to underwrite protracted military operations, various emperors since Marcus Aurelius had debased the currency to make the money go further. Ancient coins carried no mark designating what the coin was worth; instead, a coin's value depended upon the amount of valuable metal in it, determined at the moment of transaction either by roughly estimating it by hand or by weighing it on a scale. To stretch the supply of precious metals, a number of emperors reduced the amount of valuable metal in their coins, replacing it with lead, copper, or bronze.

This worked for a time, but bankers, merchants, and other money handlers soon caught on and adjusted their prices accordingly. When this happened, prices rose, even though the government tried to mandate value by law. During the reign of Septimius Severus, for instance, the amount of silver in the denarius decreased by half and was replaced by copper; by 235, the weight of a "silver" denarius had been reduced by half again; and by 275 only 2 percent of a denarius was silver. As a result, between 211, when Septimius Severus died, and 275, prices rose to twenty times their original level, an inflation rate of 2,000 percent. In time, even the government tax collectors refused to take coins, demanding that taxes be paid in kind.

To compound the problem of inflation, the cities, traditionally the heart of the Empire's economy, suffered a profound decline. While the barbarian raids—and the fear of them—were a factor, the chief culprits were the Romans themselves, who destroyed some of their greatest cities in the frequent civil wars that erupted over the choice of emperors. Septimius Severus sacked Antioch, Neapolis (in Palestine), and Byzantium while defeating competitors for the throne. If a city's confines were not breached by a passing imperial hopeful or barbarian horde, the surrounding lands supporting it might be plundered or torched and the citizens left destitute.

The cities also suffered when the traditional municipal leaders found it at first difficult and then impossible to remain. These *decurions* were government agents who collected taxes, a desirable position because they were allowed to collect a fee as well, which was added to each citizen's tax assessment. In hard times, the decurions found it harder and harder to collect taxes. Under the law, they were responsible for the amount that they were designated to collect: in case of a shortfall, the decurions had to pay it out of their own pockets. Many such individuals simply abandoned the towns and moved to their country villas, where they had no municipal responsibilities. The villas were cheaper to fortify and protect with a group of armed retainers, and they could be maintained by a few agricultural workers.

Most of the denizens of towns in western Europe at this time found it necessary to build substantial defensive walls, and Rome itself was no exception. In 271, the emperor Aurelian began construction of the impressive walls named for him, but they were not completed until 280 under his successor, Probus. This wall, which still winds through Rome, was originally twenty-five feet (7.5m) high and twelve feet (3.5m) thick; made of concrete faced with red brick, it withstood sieges of the city well into the fifteenth century.

By 284, the Empire was tottering. Although Aurelian and Probus had made needed reforms during their brief reigns, these reforms were too little too late. Neither emperor lived long enough to ensure that his changes actually did what they were supposed to do. What was needed was an emperor with ideas and the ability to stay alive long enough to institutionalize them.

THE EMPIRE REANIMATED: DIOCLETIAN

The reign of Gaius Aurelius Valerius Diocletianus (r. 285–305) would literally bring Rome back from the brink of disintegration. Diocletian was one of those rare individuals whose personal abilities allowed him to mold the times he lived in—he was, in the popular phrase, the right man at the right time.

Diocletian's first task was to organize the army in such a way as to enable it to keep the borders of the Empire secure. As a staff officer under both Aurelian and Probus, he had observed their deployment of a mobile field army, composed mainly of cavalry, to counter multiple invasions along the frontier. He had also observed, however, that the time it took for the field armies to arrive allowed raiders to penetrate deeply into Roman territory and wreak massive devastation. He set to creating a defensive system adequate to the present danger.

DIOCLETIAN'S NEW ARMY

The emperor's plan was to train three different kinds of troops and a new type of frontier fortification. Along the frontier, he stationed second-rate troops in first-rate fortifications with thick stone walls. These walls supported a number of towers that jutted out from the walls so that the soldiers within could sight along the line of the attacking enemy. Well provisioned and protected by deep ditches, Diocletian's fortresses, manned with soldiers throwing rocks and darts, were more formidable than anything earlier Roman frontier forces had used. Such structures could withstand long sieges, and the troops, composed of older soldiers, barbarian allies, and local militia, did not need the extensive training required to perform the elaborate field maneuvers of the regular Roman legions because their task was simply to defend a circuit of walls. The enemy could certainly go around these fortresses, but to do so left their supply lines vulnerable to attack.

Some miles behind these frontier forts, larger fortresses doubling as granaries were built at crossroads, fords, major towns, and other geographic choke points that invading enemies could not safely ignore. Ancient armies needed large quantities of food supplies and thus generally campaigned only after the harvest season, when they could live off the crops of the lands they invaded. Storing crops in these fortresses forced the enemy to attack them, slowing the invaders down and allowing the second part of Diocletian's defensive system to come into play.

This was a special cavalry unit called a *vexilatio*, which numbered about five hundred men often using different weapons according to their geographic location. It was their task to strike at an invader already slowed by the silo-fortresses. Often these bands of well-trained horsemen were enough to stop an invasion by themselves. If not, then fifty to eighty miles (80.5 to 129km) behind the frontier were the traditional Roman legions, still trained to a fine edge in classic Roman war maneuvers. Diocletian increased the number of these legions, adding between fourteen and twenty-four (the sources do not agree on the exact number) to the thirty-nine that served during the reign of Aurelian. These legions, operating in conjunction with the vexilationes, could be counted upon to stop any invader. In total, Diocletian added about 150,000 men to an army that had numbered 300,000 when he became emperor.

These elaborate defenses cost money, and Diocletian created an elaborate new system of taxation to get it. First, he reformed the currency, issuing a new twenty-five-denarius coin with a substantial and unvarying silver content. He also ordered that the earlier, adulterated coins be strictly valued by their precious metal content. Later, he issued a new gold coin, the aureus, and a new silver coin, the argenteus, both with fixed values. For small transactions, he issued a set of new bronze coins. With a few minor fluctuations in weight, his gold coins and the honest principles governing their issue were maintained after Diocletian's death. Roman gold coins were so pure that they were accepted outside the borders of the Empire, and examples have been found as far away as Sri Lanka.

Even with the monetary reforms, however, inflation continued. Unaware that issuing new coins and increasing the money supply can also create inflation, Diocletian blamed it on dishonest merchants. In 301, he promulgated an imperial edict setting maximum prices for every conceivable product and ordered that

his edict, carved in stone, be placed in marketplaces throughout the Empire.

DIOCLETIAN'S TAX REVOLUTION

Diocletian's most impressive economic innovation was his survey of all productive land and industry in the Empire and the assessment of taxes on the basis of that survey, according to a common measurement of productivity called by various names in various parts of the Empire, usually either *caput* ("head") or *jugum* ("yoke"). Manufactured items could also be assessed according to the *jugum* or *caput* system.

Unfortunately, the system presented inherent problems, not least that farms and industries do not produce consistently. If a farmer left his farm or if an artisan stopped or changed production, then the calculations for a specific area were no longer valid. Diocletian decreed that all workers were frozen in their occupations; a son was now required by law to follow in his father's footsteps. Such a draconian measure is shocking to our modern sense of individual initiative and success, but people back then resented it, too: almost before the Empire-wide survey was complete, people were trying to evade it. This structure, however, would endure through the Middle Ages in Europe.

The second flaw in the system was that the local magistrates, who had been victimized by earlier systems of taxation, were still

The Decline of the
Roman Empire

than a man on horseback. Diocletian's solution was an emperor for the west and another for the east, an idea that may have been suggested by the example, among others, of the emperor Carinus (r. 283–284), who was coruler with his brother Mumerianus (r. 283–284), the man whom Diocletian had succeeded.

THE TETRARCHY

Diocletian envisioned a permanent division of the Empire with a built-in system of succession. In 286, he named Marcus Aurelius Valerius Maximianus (r. 286–305, 306–308) as his coemperor, with authority over the western part of the Empire, while Diocletian himself would rule the east. Both he and Maximian bore the title "augustus." In 293, Diocletian further modified the system by naming two "caesars," one, Flavius Valerius Constantius, to serve under Maximian, and another, Gaius Galerius, to serve under himself. Each augustus adopted his caesar, gave him one of his daughters in marriage, then assigned him a portion of his part of the Empire to govern. In effect, the Empire was now divided in four parts, each with its own ruler and capital. The augustus would train his caesar and then, after twenty years, abdicate, whereupon his caesar would succeed him as augustus. At that point, the new augustus would appoint a new caesar and the process would begin anew.

This was the famous Tetrarchy, so called from tetra, the Greek word for "four." Diocletian intended for his system not only to distribute the burden of governing the Empire but also to ensure an orderly succession, thus eliminating the murderous rounds of civil wars.

Initially, the Tetrarchy seemed successful, at least in foreign affairs, for all four men performed well in their separate areas. Constantius put down a rebellion in Gaul and drove back a Frankish invasion across the

Above: This statue of the Four Tetrarchs, slightly larger than life size, is sculpted out of red porphyry stone and stands against the southwest corner of St. Mark's in Venice. In front stands the figures of the two caesars Constantius I and Galerius. Behind them stand the augusti Diocletian and Maximian.

responsible for collecting the taxes and for any shortfalls, regardless of natural disasters or losses to an invader. Nevertheless, the system worked well enough to fulfill Diocletian's purpose, which was to bring money into the military coffers and support the complex system of strong points and mobile reserves that brought peace, albeit an uneasy one, to the borders.

Autocratic though he was, Diocletian realized that the Empire was far too unwieldy for one man to rule. In the tumultuous times in which he lived, it took six weeks to move an army from Italy to Gaul and six months to Syria, and messages could travel no faster

Rhine. His resounding victory against the Germans in 298 at Langres pacified that frontier for a generation. In 296, he crossed into Britain, restored Roman rule, and created a powerful fleet to protect the island from the attacks of Saxon raiders. His fleet was the first recorded use of camouflage in history, for the hulls of the ships, their sails, and even the sailors' uniforms were greenish blue—sea-colored—to facilitate their sneaking up on Saxon warships.

Meanwhile, in the east, between 293 and 296, Galerius defeated the Goths, Sarmatians, and Marcomanni in Pannonia and Moesia (modern Yugoslavia and Bulgaria, respectively). In 298, he defeated the Persian Sasanid king Narsus at Erzerum, in eastern Turkey, and then advanced into Mesopotamia, took the town of Ctesiphon, and captured Narsus' wives and children. The peace treaty that Galerius imposed on the Sasanids resulted in fifty years of peace between the two empires. These able subordinates allowed Diocletian to continue his reforms, with Maximian implementing them in the west.

DIVINE MAJESTY

The most radical and far-reaching of Diocletian's changes was his transformation of the Roman government into an absolute monarchy. Diocletian intentionally aped the royal ceremonies of the Sasanids: both he and Maximian were to be revered as gods; their official portraits even sported halos. Diocletian created complex court rituals at his capital city of Nicomedia in northern Asia Minor. Visitors lucky enough to be admitted to the augustus' presence were expected to prostrate themselves and kiss the hem of his robes upon arising. Official appearances outside the palace, let alone in another city, required elaborate preparations, hundreds of

attendants, magnificent banners, splendid vehicles, and a slow, dignified processional.

These ceremonies were not entirely Diocletian's invention: Aurelian, an emperor in whose entourage Diocletian had served, had instituted such practices in order to impress upon the people and foreign dignitaries the divine nature of the emperor. This exalted nature would, it was hoped, protect the ruler from assassination, since his identity as a god made killing him not just treason but sacrilege. (The strategy failed Aurelian, who was killed by some of his officers.)

REORGANIZATION

In addition to economic, military, and ceremonial reforms, Diocletian completely reorganized the administration of the Empire. Fearing that provincial governors might be catalysts for rebellion, he drastically increased the number of provinces from 50 to 101 by decreasing their sizes and thus the resources available to potential rebels. The provinces were grouped into thirteen administrative districts called dioceses, each ruled by a *vicarius*, or vicar, who answered to one of four praetorian prefects, assistants to either an augustus or a caesar.

Except for a few troops that acted as police in each province, no governor or vicar commanded any military forces; the armies stationed in the provinces were under the leadership of professional military men called duces, from which the word "duke" comes. (In the 1920s and 1930s, the Italian fascist dictator Benito Mussolini, in a deliberate reference to the Roman Empire, adopted the title of duce.) In especially active areas, several duces might be supervised by a comes, or count.

ABDICATION

By 301, all of Diocletian's reforms were in place. He ruled for an additional four years and then did the unthinkable—he abdicated. Although his own Tetrarchy mandated it, it must have seemed impossible to the Roman world and beyond that he would give up absolute power. Yet Diocletian realized that if he wished the Empire to escape the evils of constant civil war, he would have to give his system a chance to work. During his reign he had built an elaborate palace at Salona (modern Split), to which he retired after he left office on May 1, 305. Diocletian forced Maximian to do the same in Milan. With great pomp and ceremony both men transferred their imperial power to the two caesars, Galerius and Constantius. Diocletian lived another eleven years happily isolated from government affairs in his gigantic palace complex, where he grew turnips and cabbages.

He lived long enough to see portions of his reform destroyed and no doubt died thinking he had failed. Yet he was wise enough to resist a call from his old colleague, Maximian, who in 306 attempted to come out of retirement and resume power.

FRAGMENTATION IN THE EMPIRE

Almost immediately, things began to unravel. While Diocletian's successors realized the wisdom of his economic and military reforms, they rejected the Tetrarchy. Sharing power did not fit into the philosophy of any of the emperors who followed Diocletian. Once Diocletian stepped down, the Empire was convulsed by civil war. Gaius Galerius, Diocletian's successor in the east, faced a number of claimants to the throne in the west, including Constantius, the legitimate augustus in the west, and, after Constantius' untimely death in 306, the latter's son, Constantine; the aged ex-emperor Maximian, bored by retirement and anxious to resume power; and finally Maxentius, Maximian's son.

After the death of Galerius in 310, the situation worsened. Galerius' legitimate successor in the eastern part of the Empire was Maximinus Daia, but in the west not Maxentius in Italy nor Constantine in Trier (a German city on the Moselle River) nor another claimant, Valerius Licinianus Licinius in the Balkans, acknowledged him. In 312, Constantine simplified things by advancing against Maxentius and defeating him at the famous Battle of the Milvian Bridge on October 28. It was here, according to Christian legend, that on the night before the battle Constantine had a dream that told him to instruct his soldiers to paint the Greek letters *chi rho* (standing for *Christus*, or Christ) on their shields. Constantine attributed his subsequent victory to Christ, and in 313, in gratitude, he issued the Edict of Milan, which officially recognized Christianity and restored property to the church that had been confiscated earlier. In the same year, near Adrianople in northern Greece, Licinius defeated Maximinus Daia, thus eliminating him from the competition for the Empire.

Constantine I and the Triumph of Christianity

Constantine and Licinius now ruled the Roman world between them, and for a time, each unsure of the other's strength, they mutually tolerated each other. But in 324, the uneasy peace ended. Constantine's army and navy defeated Licinius' forces both at Adrianople and at the mouth of the Dardanelles. When Constantine later captured Licinius in Asia Minor, he found himself master of the whole Roman world.

Once in power, Constantine made changes in Diocletian's system while preserving much of it. First to go was the Tetrarchy, which Constantine felt courted rebellion, though he maintained the division of the Empire into four administrative units, replacing the augusti and caesars with four prefects, each of whom governed a fourth of the Empire in Constantine's name. When Constantine died, his successors kept this system but also added an

arrangement whereby the rule of the Empire was split between two close relatives. For instance, Constantine's son and successor, Constantius II (r. 337–361), ruled in conjunction with his brothers, Constantine II (r. 337–340) and Constans (r. 340–350). When Constans died, Constantius II coruled with Gallus (r. 350–354), his nephew.

In the immediate aftermath of Constantine's death, the expectation that blood ties might somehow blunt the desire for power proved unrealistic: Constantine's sons all sought to murder each other for political gain.

If Constantine did not see the value of the Tetrarchy, he certainly appreciated Diocletian's tax which provided Constantine with the money he needed to support both the army and the government. Yet he kept only part of the monetary reforms that accompanied that system. He abandoned sound silver coinage, though he continued Diocletian's sound gold coinage. His reasoning was simple: gold was the metal of the rich and of international trade and diplomacy. As far as he was concerned, the poor could pay their taxes in

kind and manage their paltry affairs with an unsound copper coinage.

Constantine also altered Diocletian's defensive military structure. For reasons of economy and security of the throne, he combined the numerous legions and vexilationes that Diocletian had stationed behind the frontier into one large field army under the personal control of the emperor. From that time on, the frontier garrisons were expected to hold until they were relieved by the field army. After Constantine's death, in the years of the two coemperors, each one had a field army to protect his half of the Empire. Constantine's arrangement was not only cheaper, but it ensured that the emperor, at the head of the main fighting force of the Empire, could protect himself better from revolts. The downside of the arrangement was that the regions behind the frontier now had to endure periodic plundering by invaders until the main army arrived.

Constantine made a radical change in the army when he began to actively recruit promising Germans for high-command positions in the army. Not only were these men excellent soldiers, but they had come from a society where soldiers traditionally had a special relationship of trust with their leader. Constantine undoubtedly saw this personal allegiance as the best guarantee against revolution and assassination.

He maintained virtually unchanged the ceremonial system that Diocletian had created. The emperor still attempted to overawe his subjects and foreign visitors with an impressive ritualized display of opulent wealth and supreme power. Nowhere was this more evident than in Constantine's great construction of the Empire's new capital on the ancient site of Byzantium. He named his new city New Rome when he founded it in 330, and he laid it out like Rome by dividing it into fourteen districts and delineating seven "hills" within its boundaries.

He even instituted a Senate, whose lack of real political power matched that of its counterpart in Rome.

THE EQUAL OF THE APOSTLES

Constantine's significant departure from Diocletian's ceremonial system was to present himself not as a living god, but as the representative on earth of the Living God of the Christians. As such, he made himself the final arbiter and supervisor of the Christian clergy within the Empire. In 315, after the Christians had failed to reach a decision on a question of doctrine at the Synod of Arles, Constantine rendered a decision from the throne.

In 325, he presided over the crucial Council of Nicaea, which determined the official Christian doctrine of the Trinity, the date of Easter, and the structure of the Church hierarchy. These actions made him, in official Church doctrine, an Isopostolos, or the Equal of the Apostles. Analogously with Diocletian's system, his new position made revolt against him not only secular treason but also treason against God, exposing the guilty not only to punishment on earth but to eternal damnation. No rebel against the Roman government had ever faced such drastic retribution.

CONSTANTINE THE MAN

Bishop Eusebius of Caesarea, who knew the emperor, left a vivid description of him. We know Constantine was a robust, well-built man renowned for his strength and pleasing appearance. He was equally noted for his violent temper, suspicious nature, and overdependence on informers, all qualities that would lead to personal tragedy when, in 326, he ordered the execution of his own son Crispus on a charge of treason.

The official charge, according to the contemporary historian Zosimus, was that Crispus had attempted to seduce his stepmother, Fausta, who reported the attempt to Constantine. Another contemporary historian, Sidonius Apollinaris, claims that Fausta entered willingly into an affair with her stepson, then turned on Crispus, reporting the affair as a rape in order to get Crispus out of the way so that one of her own three sons by Constantine might succeed to the throne. If that was her plan, Fausta achieved her goal, for all three eventually became emperor.

Unfortunately for Fausta, several months after the execution, Constantine's mother, Helena, discovered the deception and reported it to Constantine. Enraged, Constantine had Fausta scalded to death in her bath. Helena herself may have been seeking revenge against Fausta because Fausta's mother, Theodora, had broken up Helena's marriage to Constantius I twenty years before. Lacking the opportunity to make Theodora pay, Helena vented her anger on the daughter.

HOLDING THE BORDERS

The Roman Empire had undergone remarkable changes in the century and a half between the death of Marcus Aurelius to that of Constantine. The Empire had nearly succumbed to the relentless pressure of invading barbarians from outside the frontier, while within its borders the emperors had faced the constant threat of revolution and assassination. They held the frontiers despite these threats due to a combination of personal bravery, the fighting skill of the Roman soldier, the poor discipline of the barbarians, and constantly updated military policies and strategies.

Diocletian's thorough reorganization of the Empire's government, economy, and military structure contributed greatly to the Empire's survival, reinforced by the timely succession of the capable Constantine. Constantine's shifting of the center of government to Constantinople ensured that the eastern part of the Empire would survive for another thousand years. No less important was his legalization of Christianity, making possible an alliance between church and state that would later reinforce the stability of the Empire in the east. At the end of Constantine's reign, the government was strong, if autocratic, and the frontiers were firm. Unfortunately, new elements among the barbarian tribes outside the Empire now threatened it once more.

Above: Peter Paul Rubens painted this work showing the emblem of Christ appearing to Constantine. Although some ancient sources state that the *chi rho* letters of Christ's name appeared to Constantine in a dream, other sources claim they appeared in the sky the night before the battle.

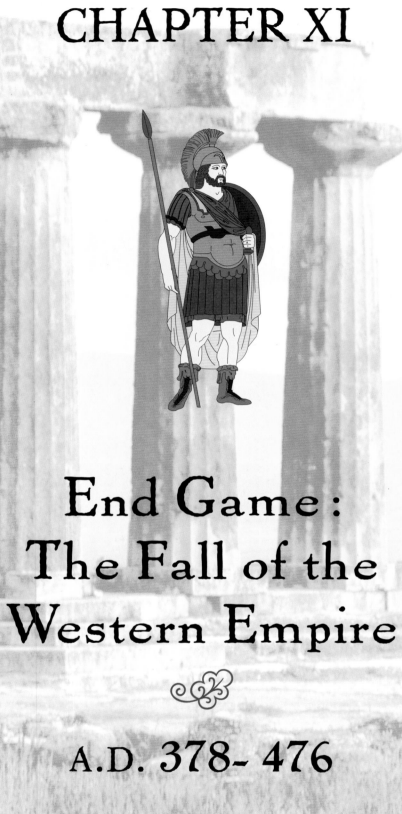

CHAPTER XI

End Game: The Fall of the Western Empire

A.D. 378- 476

Pages 160–161: Famous for the early Christian mosaics of its churches, Ravenna, on the Adriatic coast of Italy, became the capital of the western Roman Empire in 402 when the military threat of the Visigoths impelled the emperor Honorius to move the capital there. This mosaic in the Church of San Apollinare Nuovo depicts Saints Peter and Paul adoring the throne of Christ.

FAR TO THE EAST OF THE Roman frontiers, on the great sweeping steppes of Asia, a barbarian people called the Huns began to ride westward about A.D. 100. Over the years, they displaced other barbarians, who in turn displaced others and so on until finally, in 378, the Visigoths, the westernmost tribes, pushed their way into the Roman Empire by being pressed from behind. From that year on, wave after wave of barbarians moved against the Roman frontiers. The Roman armies fought back valiantly, while the emperors exhausted their financial and diplomatic resources to stop the flow.

By the mid-fifth century, however, the barbarians had flooded the western part of the Empire, causing its final collapse. By this time, barbarians controlled the city of Rome itself: the first barbarian king of Rome, the German Odoacer (r. 476–493), pulled the last Roman emperor off the throne and sent the imperial paraphernalia to the Roman emperor of the east, who was ruling in Constantinople. Western Europe had entered a new era.

AFTER CONSTANTINE

At Constantine's death, the Hunnish threat was still in the future. The emperor's military reforms had won a twenty-year respite from barbarian invasions, leaving his heirs free to squabble over the succession. In the months following his death in 337, his sons, the three principal contenders for the throne, massacred all of their distant relatives. These three heirs then carved up the Empire among them: Constantine II received Gaul, Spain, and Britain; Constantius II, Italy and Illyricum (roughly modern Bosnia, Croatia, and Slovenia); and Constans, Asia, Egypt, and the rest of Africa. By 354, Constantius II was in overall command of the Empire, and he found it necessary to appoint two of his nephews, Gallus Flavius Claudius Constantius and Flavius Claudius Julianus, to assist him as caesars because by then foreign forces were once again threatening the Empire.

Julian went west to deal with the incursions of the Franks, a Germanic tribe, across the Rhine; he won a resounding victory and recruited twenty thousand of the former enemy into the Roman army. Julian's success fed his popularity, and a jealous Constantius decided to eliminate him. The two cousins led their armies against each other, but Constantius died, and Julian became emperor in 361.

His reign of only two years was an enlightened one: so effectively did he reform the tax-collection system, ensuring greater honesty, that he was able to lower taxes. Raised as a Christian, his philosophical studies brought him to embrace his pagan heritage—for having abandoned his earlier religious practice, he is known in history as Julian the Apostate. Though his official policy was one of religious toleration, he employed his imperial power to benefit pagan cults and withdraw some of the privileges that Constantine had extended to the Christians. So strong was his anti-Christian bias that it intimidated even some of his pagan subjects, while his proposed legislation aimed at reinstating paganism as the official religion of the Empire earned him enemies among the Christians. Finally, during a battle with the Persians in June 363, an unknown Christian murdered him.

End Game:
The Fall of the Western Empire

Left: Julian attempted to restore paganism as the Empire's dominant religion when he unexpectedly became emperor in 361. He tried to discourage Christianity by the nonviolent means of abolishing its tax-exempt status and removing Christians from positions of imperial authority. His potential success will never be known, because he was murdered, according to legend, by one of his Christian soldiers during a battle against the Parthians. His famous last words, "Galilean [his term for Jesus], you have conquered!" supposedly signified his deathbed realization that his campaign against the Church had failed.

End Game :
The Fall of the Western Empire

Left without an emperor at a critical time, a caucus of officers elected one of their own, Jovian, a devout Christian, to replace the slain Julian, but in February 364, after the conclusion of the war against Persia, Jovian was asphyxiated in his sleep by fumes from a charcoal stove. Another caucus of generals then elected Flavius Valentinianus, who almost immediately appointed his brother Valens as coemperor. Right away Valentinian set out for Gaul to protect the frontier and campaigned successfully against the Germans on the Rhine frontier, while a trusted general, Theodosius Flavius, subdued Britain and Africa. By the time Valentinian died in 375, the borders of the Empire were once more secure.

THE VISIGOTHS

Three years later, the apparent calm along the frontier shattered when 200,000 Visigoths, fifty thousand of them warriors, broke through the frontier north of Adrianople and raided throughout the Balkan peninsula. Valens rushed north to meet them, while his nephew Gratian (r. 367–383), Valentinian's son, who ruled the western half of the Empire, hurried east with reinforcements. At the Battle of Adrianople on August 9, 378, twenty thousand Roman soldiers died, along with Valens himself; the Roman defeat was the result of the emperor's unwise decision, motivated perhaps by a desire for personal glory, to engage the Visigoths before Gratian's troops could arrive.

Still, the training and discipline of the Roman army allowed the Empire to survive even this massive loss. In 379, Gratian appointed Theodosius I (r. 378–395) to succeed Valens, and Theodosius lost no time rebuilding the army and leading a vigorous campaign against the Visigoths. To fill the army's ranks he pressed thousands of conscripts into service, and he launched a three-year campaign against the Visigoths that was ultimately successful.

FROM ENEMIES TO ALLIES

Once they were defeated, the settlement Theodosius reached with the Visigoths was a departure from earlier ones. Where previously victorious emperors took some barbarians into the army, training them in Roman methods of warfare, Theodosius, perhaps feeling less assured of his victory than earlier conquerors, granted lenient terms to the Visigoths. They were settled in Moesia as *foederati*, or allies, meaning that they did not become an integral part of the Roman army or adopt its training and equipment. As allies, they held Moesia as a kind of client kingdom, running their own affairs, paying no taxes, and living under their own laws. They promised only to fight as auxiliary forces of the Roman army when asked.

Not all of Theodosius' contemporaries agreed with his terms. Bishop Synesius of Ptolemais in Palestine felt that the policy reflected weakness and created a dangerous precedent; history proved him correct. In the next century, as more and more barbarian tribes were admitted as foederati, the western part of the Empire became a fragmented federation of a dozen barbarian kingdoms interspersed among Roman territories. By around 450, the only areas of western Europe still under direct Roman control were Italy itself and portions of the provinces of Raetia and Noricum (roughly modern Switzerland and Austria, respectively).

The barbarian chieftains that led these groups were not necessarily anti-Roman; most actively sought and were proud to receive the recognition of the

Roman emperor. Reverence for the traditions and former grandeur of Rome was not the only reason for the barbarian leaders' deference.

Another was Christianity, which by the early fourth century was an active presence within the Empire. At the very time the barbarians were invading the Empire, Christian missionaries were rapidly converting them. The Visigoths who slaughtered the Romans at Adrianople were killing fellow Christians. To these peoples, Christianity offered certain advantages, not the least of which, as the barbarians took over the Empire's complex but lucrative administrative and tax systems, was the literacy of the Christian clerics.

BARBARIAN POWER WITHIN THE EMPIRE

The borders remained quiet for the remainder of Theodosius' reign; his greatest problem was now internal rebellions. When Theodosius' own army murdered his coemperor, Gratian, in 383, on the German frontier, the troops chose as emperor Magnus Maximus, a successful Roman general in Britain. As emperor in the east, Theodosius threw his support behind the embattled western emperor Valentinian II (r. 375–392). In a whirlwind campaign in 387, Theodosius marched into Italy, defeated Magnus Maximus, and established Valentinian II on the throne.

Five years later, Valentinian II was murdered by a Frank whom some sources call Arbogast and who had been one of Valentinian's own generals. These generals placed Eugenius, an apostate Christian, on the throne, provoking Theodosius, a zealous Christian, to lead an army back to the west in 394 to defeat those whom he saw as the forces of darkness—both politically and religiously. The battle on the Frigidus River

(in modern Slovenia, near its border with Italy) demonstrated, at least to the superstitious minds of the fourth century, the power of Christianity. Theodosius attacked Arbogast's camp on September 5 but was driven back with heavy losses.

The next day, after a night of prayer, he foolishly attacked once more, against the advice of his own officers. Yet at the moment of apparent defeat, when his army faltered and began to fall back, a miraculous wind suddenly swept out of the mountains, blew dust into the eyes of Arbogast's men, and literally pushed Theodosius' attack into their blinded ranks. When

Above: During the period from the rise of Theodosius I to the death of Honorius (A.D. 378–421), the Roman imperial general Stilicho—seen here in a carving on an ivory diptych—served as advisor and commander of the western Roman army. He was instrumental in defeating the Visigoth king Alaric in 402.

End Game:
The Fall of the Western Empire

Arbogast's troops broke and ran, it seemed a sure sign of the victory of the Christian Theodosius over the pagans.

Although he was defeated and killed, Arbogast was representative of the growing influence that Germanic officers began to have in the Roman army—an influence that would become even more apparent during the reign of Honorius (r. 395–423) and Arcadius (r. 395–408), the sons of Theodosius who became coemperors when Theodosius died in 395.

The two emperors were still young when they began their joint rule; Honorius was only ten and Arcadius eighteen. The son of a Vandal chieftain, Stilicho, one of Theodosius' advisors and generals, was the most important influence upon the two young rulers; until Stilicho's death in 408, as regent for Honorius, he was effectively ruler in the west. It was Stilicho who perpetuated Theodosius' legacy in the west, including the spread of Christianity and the continued settlement of barbarians on Roman land as foederati. He often found himself in conflict with Arcadius' advisors in the east, who saw Stilicho as a rival who wanted to control the entire Empire.

In an environment increasingly beset by barbarian forces, Stilicho thought it best for Honorius to leave his capital at Milan—Rome had not been an imperial residence since before Diocletian—and retreat to Ravenna, on the Adriatic coast of Italy, where the court would be defended by deep swamps and difficult terrain.

Indeed, between 406 and 408, the western portion of the Empire faced overwhelming attacks from which it never recovered. On the Rhine frontier, a Roman army had been holding out against a combined attack of Suevi, Alans, and Vandals. An important part of their defensive strategy included warships adapted to fight along the Rhine, but on the night of December 31, 406, the Rhine froze solid and 100,000 barbarians swarmed into central Gaul. The defenders were overrun, and the province lost in less than a month.

ALARIC

On the heels of that devastating defeat, Honorius accused Stilicho of treason and ordered his execution. In 395, upon Theodosius' death, Alaric, a Visigoth king, left Roman service and invaded Greece until Arcadius placated him by making Alaric governor of Illyricum. In 401, Alaric had invaded Italy until Stilicho drove him back. Now, with Stilicho dead, Alaric saw an opportunity to invade Italy once more, and this time he was successful. His army swept down into central Italy, destroyed all opposition, and arrived outside the walls of Rome in November 408.

The city was safe from immediate danger, because by this time no army, barbarian or Roman, had preserved the capability of siege warfare. While Honorius lolled in Ravenna, Alaric ranged the countryside and pillaged to feed his army. Repeated negotiations failed because he demanded every piece of gold and silver in the city. Things became so des-

Above: Daughter of Theodosius I (r. 378–395) and sister to Honorius, Galla Placidia was one of the most powerful women of the late Roman Empire. Supposedly, this jeweled cross was part of a vast nuptial gift given to her by her barbarian husband, Ataulf, after she was captured by the Visigoths in 410. Despite a forced marriage she grew to love Ataulf, and when he was murdered by a usurper named Singeric, Galla Placidia avenged her husband's death by arranging for Singeric's murder.

perate that Pope Innocent not only encouraged the Christians in Rome to pray but authorized the few remaining pagans in Rome to practice their long-banned sacrificial rites.

The efforts to pray for the salvation of the city was to no avail, however, for during the night of August 24, 410, someone inside Rome opened the **Salarian Gate** and Alaric's horde streamed in. He allowed his troops to sack the city for three days and then withdrew, since there was not enough food for his men in Rome. Alaric led his army south toward the "toe" of Italy, where he gathered a fleet to take him across to Sicily. A storm, which the Christians immediately ascribed to divine intervention, wrecked the ships and Alaric turned north, but he died on the way.

Alaric's soldiers ordered their Roman prisoners of war to divert the course of a small stream, the Busento.

A tomb was constructed and adorned lavishly with many Roman spoils. After burying Alaric in the stream's bed, the Visigoths restored the Busento to its original course, then killed the prisoners who had provided the labor for this task. Alaric's brother-in-law, Ataulf, the Visigoths' new leader, led the army out of Italy. In 412, Ataulphus' successor, Vallia, accepted to become foederatus and settled in Gaul.

Meanwhile, the Empire in the west was disintegrating. The Suevi, Alans, and Vandals, who had crossed the Rhine in 406, poured into Gaul and continued southward into Spain. The Vandals moved across to Africa in 436, where they became foederati in Mauretania and Numidia. In Britain, the Romans had withdrawn to meet the invaders on the continent in 406 and never returned. The island broke down into a number of small kingdoms.

End Game:
The Fall of the Western Empire

THE LAST DAYS OF THE EMPIRE

The western portion of the Empire would stage one last resurgence, led by Honorius; his half-sister, Galla Placidia; and Flavius Aetius, the last great Roman general. The three of them cobbled together a new political order based on the foederati system. Although the actual power of the "Roman" government at this time did not extend outside of Italy, barbarian leaders in Gaul, Spain, North Africa, and parts of Noricum and Pannonia (modern Austria and Hungary, respectively) recognized the leadership of the western Roman emperor and—most importantly—promised to fight for it.

Galla Placidia (c. 390–450), an extraordinary personage, was Ataulf's widow when she married Constantius III, Honorius' coemperor for seven months in 421. When Honorius died of natural causes in 423, Galla Placidia placed Valentinian III, her son with Constantius III, on the throne. Valentinian III (r. 423–455) was an ineffective monarch who left the important decisions to his mother and to Aetius, the commander of his army. During Valentinian's reign, the western part of the

End Game:
The Fall of the Western Empire

168

End Game:
The Fall of the Western Empire

Empire met its final challenge with the invasion of the Huns; the Empire emerged victorious but too weak to survive.

ATTILA THE HUN

While Stilicho and Alaric were struggling for power, the Huns had settled as foederati in Pannonia; Arcadius had kept them happy with huge payments in gold. In 433, Attila (r. 434–453), with his brother Bleda, became king of the Huns; around 445, Attila had Bleda murdered. The Huns periodically raided territories in the eastern, or Byzantine, Empire, and in 447 they forced both Arcadius' son Theodosius II (r. 408–450) and Valentinian III to increase their yearly payments. In 450 that changed when Marcian (r. 450–457), the new emperor in Constantinople, flatly refused to pay. Encouraged by Marcian's bold example, the western Empire refused, too.

Attila immediately attacked the western Empire, well aware that it was the weaker. Sometime in early 451, Attila moved west out of Pannonia toward Gaul, gathering Ostrogoths and Burgundians. Crossing the Rhine, he took Cologne, Rheims, Mainz, Metz, and Strasbourg. When the walls of Paris proved too strong, he turned south and laid siege to Orleans. In the meantime, Aetius was approaching from the south, and in June the two armies met outside of Chalons, some thirty miles (48km) south of Rheims.

The losses on both sides must have been staggering because when the dust settled, neither army advanced. Aetius stayed in place while Attila retreated south into Italy seeking to feed his army as it marched against Rome. At the same time, Marcian dispatched an army from the east to help defend Rome. By the time Attila was approaching the city, he was menaced by Marcian's army, and by the possibility that Aetius

and an unnamed plague compounded by famine might follow him.

Pope Leo I (r. 440–461), who had organized the defenses of the city, used these natural phenomena to his advantage when he met with Attila outside the walls. He convinced the profoundly superstitious Attila that it was the Christian god who had sent both plague and famine to punish the Huns. Attila called off the attack and retreated. He died two years later from a severe nosebleed while celebrating his marriage to a Burgundian princess. The Huns, unable to find an effective leader to replace Attila, were crushed by a confederation of Herules, Goths, and Suevi.

The Battle of Chalons was equally devastating to the Romans. Perhaps Aetius could have rebuilt the army, but in 454, he was killed during an argument with Valentinian III, who was in turn assassinated by two of Aetius' barbarian bodyguards.

THE LAST EMPERORS

With no army and no effective leader, the Empire of the west lurched toward its end. With one exception, its last eight emperors between 454 and 476 were weak and shadowy figures, dominated by Germanic generals who used them as figureheads and set them up and pulled them down at will. The exception was Anthemius (r. 467–472), who was briefly able to prevent further deterioration of the Roman power in Gaul by recruiting effective Germanic leaders to serve as Roman foederati.

At the same time that Anthemius was struggling to hold central Gaul against the Visigoths, he had to fight the Vandal Gaiseric (r. 428–477), who ruled a good portion of the North African coast. In 455, Gaiseric and his Vandals had sacked Rome; this time, Pope Leo's appeals had fallen on deaf ears, and he had been able to extract from Gaiseric only a promise not to loot the churches. From that time on, Gaiseric, his hand firmly on the African grain exports to Italy, was a constant menace to Rome.

In 468, with the help of a fleet from Marcian, Anthemius tried to dislodge Gaiseric, but Gaiseric caught the Roman fleet at sea and sank it with fire ships. Defeated, Anthemius was besieged and then killed in Rome by his own general, a Visigoth named Ricimer, who then set up Olybrius (r. 472–473) as a puppet emperor. When these two died in 473, a Burgundian king named Gundobad, Ricimer's nephew, set up Glycerius (r. 473–474) as emperor.

Leo (r. 457–474), the emperor in Constantinople, opposed to Glycerius ruling in Italy, made one of his relatives, Julius Nepos (r. 474–475), emperor in Rome. Olybrius, unwilling to face the usual fate of western emperors, offered to abdicate if he were made bishop of Salona in Illyricum. And not a moment too soon: Orestes, garrison commander in Rome, wanted to place his own son, who bore the most Roman name of Romulus Augustulus (r. 475–476), on the throne; when Julius Nepos obligingly fled the city, the boy became emperor.

Soon after, a delegation of Germanic officers approached Orestes with the shocking request that the young emperor grant their troops foederati status and lands in Italy. No such troops had ever been settled in this manner south of the Alps. Orestes refused and he was deposed as his son's regent. When the officers elected one of their own, Odoacer, to replace Orestes, Odoacer decided that it was silly to keep a young boy on the throne and simply deposed him, becoming the first barbarian king of Italy.

Romulus Augustulus must have been extremely young because Odoacer apparently thought it was

inhumane to kill him. Instead he exiled him to Campania along with his family and gave him a pension. Nothing else is known about the boy emperor except that he survived as a private citizen into the reign of Theodoric, who ruled a united Italy from 493, when he had Odoacer killed, until he died in 526.

Romulus Augustulus appeared before the Senate in Rome to surrender the imperial regalia (most likely a gown and purple garments), which the Senate accepted and forwarded with a delegation to Constantinople. The delegation presented the imperial trappings to the emperor Zeno (r. 474–491), saying that although they no longer needed an emperor in the west, they felt the Empire should be united under a single emperor—the one in the east. For a short time, Zeno made a show of demanding the reinstatement of Julius Nepos as emperor, but in the end he recognized Odoacer as his representative in Italy. The Roman Empire of the west was no more.

Below: The eagle was the traditional symbol of the power of Rome. The dictator Marius in 104 B.C. ordered that each legion put a silver eagle on the top of its standard. The loss of an eagle standard in battle often led to the disbanding of the legion. This eagle is of onyx and dates to about 40 A.D.

End Game:
The Fall of the Western Empire

Further Reading

The following list of books is by no means exhaustive, but the books are readily available, and, besides being sound scholarship, are written on a level that the layman can appreciate. The list also contains books by ancient authors that are still entertaining and informative.

Ashe, Geoffrey. *The Discovery of King Arthur*. Garden City, New Jersey: Anchor Press, 1985. Not only a good description of late Roman Britain, but an excellent book about one of the most famous characters in history.

Birley, Anthony. *Marcus Aurelius*. New Haven: Yale University Press, 1987.

Bradford, Ernle. *Hannibal*. New York: Dorset Press, 1981.

Burns, Thomas. *A History of the Ostrogoths*. Bloomington, Indiana: Indiana University Press, 1984.

Carcopino, Jerome. *Daily Life in Ancient Rome*. Translated by E.O. Lorimer. New Haven: Yale University Press, 1968 edition. Probably the best book available on how the Romans lived.

Cary, Max. *A History of Ancient Rome Down to the Reign of Constantine*. London: MacMillan and Company, 1960. The best one-volume history of Rome in print.

Cornell, Tim J. *The Beginnings of Rome*. London: Routledge Publishers, 1995.

Elton, Hugh. *Frontiers of the Roman Empire*. Bloomington, Indiana: Indiana University Press, 1996.

Eusebius of Caesarea. *The History of the Church*. Translated by G.A. Williamson. Harmondsworth, Middlesex, England: Penguin Classics, 1965.

Ferrill, Arther. *The Fall of the Roman Empire: The Military Explanation*. London: Thames and Hudson, 1986.

Finley, M.I. *Ancient Slavery and Modern Ideology*. New York: Viking Press, 1980.

Fletcher, Richard. *The Barbarian Conversions: From Paganism to Christianity A.D. 371-1386*. New York: Henry Holt and Company, 1997.

Galinsky, Karl. *Augustan Culture*. Princeton, New Jersey: Princeton University Press, 1996.

Gibbon, Edward. *The Decline and Fall of the Roman Empire*, Three Volumes. New York: The Modern Library, 1956. Even though it was written more than two centuries ago, it is still one of the best sources for the period after 180 A.D. Gibbon's style makes it a classic of English literature.

Grant, Michael. *The Etruscans*. New York: Charles Scribner's Sons, 1980.

Griffin, Miriam T. *Nero: The End of a Dynasty*. New Haven: Yale University Press, 1984.

Hornblower, Simon, and Anthony Spawforth. *The Oxford Classical Dictionary, Third Edition*. Oxford: Oxford University Press, 1996. The best single source on ancient Greece and Rome.

Jones, A.H.M. *The Decline and Fall of the Ancient World*. New York: Holt, Rinehart and Winston, 1966. The best modern study of the subject.

Le Bohec, Yann. *The Imperial Roman Army*. Translated by B.T. Batsford. New York: Hippocrene Books Inc., 1994. The most complete study of the Roman army in print.

Livius, Titus. *The Early History of Rome*. Translated by Aubrey de Selincourt. Harmondsworth, Middlesex, England: Penguin Classics, 1960.

———. *Rome and Italy*. Translated by Betty Radice. London: Penguin Classics, 1982.

MacMullen, Ramsey. *Constantine*. New York: Harper and Row Publishers, 1969.

Maenchen-Helfen, Otto J. *The World of the Huns*. Berkeley, California: University of California Press, 1973.

Moss, H. St. L.B. *The Birth of the Middle Ages 395-814*. London: Oxford University Press, 1969.

Polybius of Megalopolis. *The Rise of the Roman Empire*. Translated by Ian Scott-Kilvert. London: Penguin Classics, 1979.

Robertson, D.S. *Greek and Roman Architecture*. Cambridge: Cambridge University Press, 1971.

Smith, John Holland. *Constantine the Great*. New York: Charles Scribner's Sons, 1980.

Spivey, Nigel. *Etruscan Art*. London: Thames and Hudson, 1997.

Stambaugh, John E. *The Ancient Roman City*. Baltimore: The Johns Hopkins University Press, 1988.

Stark, Rodney. *The Rise of Christianity*. Princeton, New Jersey: Princeton University Press, 1996. An original and credible new theory about the growth of Christianity in its first four centuries.

Suetonius Tranquillus, Gaius. *The Twelve Caesars*. Translated by Robert Graves. Harmondsworth, Middlesex, England: Penguin Classics, 1957.

White, K.D. *Greek and Roman Technology*. Ithaca, New York: Cornell University Press, 1984.

Wilkin, Robert L. *The Christians as the Romans Saw Them*. New Haven: Yale University Press, 1984.

Williams, Stephen. *Diocletian and the Roman Recovery*. New York: Methane, Inc., 1985.

Index

Photo Credits